For The Children

For The Children

A Novel

Denise E. Johnson

For The Children

We extend our deepest gratitude to the countless scholars, translators, and scribes who have dedicated their lives to preserving and translating the sacred texts contained within the various version of the Bible. Their unwavering commitment to accurately transmitting the message of faith and wisdom has enriched the lives of countless individuals throughout history. We acknowledge the immense effort and dedication required to compile, translate, and disseminate these invaluable Scriptures, which serve as a beacon of guidance and inspiration to millions around the world.

Scripture quotations marked (MSG) are taken from *The Message,* copyright © 1993, 2002, 2018 by Eugene H. Peterson. Used by permission of NavPress. All rights reserved. Represented by Tyndale House Publishers. Scripture quotations marked NLT are taken from the Holy Bible, New Living Translation, copyright 1996, 2004. Used by permission of Tyndale House Publishers, Inc., Wheaton, Illinois 60189.

Disclaimer: Although *For The Children* is strictly fictitious, the circumstances written about are very real and are occurring in our country and across the globe. Names, characters, places, and incidents are products of my imagination or are used fictitiously, so any resemblance to actual events or locales or persons, living or dead, is entirely coincidental

ISBN 978-0-9984510-0-8
Library of Congress Control Number 2016920607
Denise E. Johnson, Billings, MT

Praises of
For The Children

As a Family Life Educator, CASA advocate, sexual assault advocate, and abolitionist with Operation Underground Railroad, I am familiar with how broken our child welfare system is. Conversations like the one your book opens need to happen. People from all sides of the issue need to come together to work on solutions.

    −Brittany G. Homer − CCFLE-P

This novel clearly shows what is going on with the child welfare system in our country. I could not put the book down...I was captured by the second page. EVERYONE in this country should read this book.

    −Georgia Miller - Montana Child Protection Alliance

I couldn't put *For The Children* down. As a professional who works with children and families, I could identify with every situation in this book!!! Thank you for writing this book...our mission working on behalf of children is never done!

    −Shirley Bullock - Teacher and children's mental health counselor/advocate

As a foster parent, I have been given an inside view of the broken foster care system. The children are truly voiceless. The wounds are deep and the trauma is far reaching. Thank you for writing such a well-written book!

    −Megan Richert - Foster mom and child advocate

I cannot express how impressed I am with *For The Children.* As soon as I started reading, I could not put it down. It touched on so many important issues. I hope everyone involved in children's welfare will read this book. Thank you for speaking for the children. Thank you for writing this book.

    −Laura Houser - Mom and business owner

I could not put the book down. As someone who has always worked with children and was on a state foster care review board, it was an eye opener and a tear jerker. Denise has a gift of writing. I would highly recommend it to anyone who loves children.

    −Denise Kester - Mom, grandmother, school librarian, educator

I started reading this book one evening and several hours later, found myself so engrossed in the story that I couldn't put it down. Although the book is fictional, our family experienced similar circumstances. This will stir something within you to want to learn more yourself. Great book! Thank you, Denise for writing it.

    −Roxi Burns - Mom, grandmother, entrepreneur

"*For The Children*" is a heart-wrenching novel that shares gripping stories of foster care. Denise highlights the challenges of parenting, the inability of some to continue the parenting journey, and the help many social workers and foster care families offer to a broken system. This engaging book will provide you with new understanding and awareness of our current culture as well as how to get involved to help vulnerable families, especially children. This book is well worth your time.

    −Pamela L. Strong - Author of "Anchored by Tender Mercies: Hope for those in Grief and Trauma"

Acknowledgements

Who reads this section anyway? Most people want to get right to the book. Who can blame them? If you're that person, then yes, get after it. Read *For The Children*, but then come back to this because there is some good stuff here too.

Writing is one of those things that makes you feel vulnerable. Words you've labored over are out there for everyone to love or hate, embrace or critique, but before a book ever goes to print, you need a little of all of it. Thus, you need people who are safe and honest.

I have been blessed with such people in my life. My sister Colleen has always been my biggest cheerleader, no matter what it is I am doing. After publishing my first non-fiction book *Love To Give*, she suggested I write a fiction book. My first reaction? "I don't think I could do that." Wrong thing to say to her.

Next thing I knew, she arranged a lunch date to meet with published author Susan Hill, who graciously shared nuggets of information. By the time I'd traveled the two hours home, God planted the seeds of *For The Children* into my mind. I started slow, but slow wasn't good enough for my cheerleader, who then sent me to a Christian Writers Conference at Mount Hermon in California. I arrived with a rough manuscript in hand and came home realizing I had a lot of work to do. What a wonderful experience and opportunity to learn, grow, and meet amazing people. They helped me to see how God uses those with a passion to write, to tell His stories.

So in between the craziness of life, ***For The Children*** became a reality. At points I felt stuck, so I would call Colleen for inspiration and then I'd be off again, writing and honing my craft. Therefore, I would be remiss to not give my sister credit for giving me a nudge, a shove, and sometimes a kick in the pants to keep moving. Thanks Sis. I needed it!

Thank you to my husband Ron for encouraging me and helping me through the distractions and chaos of life so I could sneak away and write. I also want to thank my children Tucker, Kassi, and Josh as well as my mom Bev for hearing out scene ideas, and giving me input along the way.

I thank Sam Lucas and his team who designed my cover and developed promotional materials to give ***For The Children*** its own identity.

Most importantly, I want to give God the glory because He gave me the story, the desire to write, connected me to people, and gave me the passion for children in our world. I hope this story brings honor and glory to Him who is the Great Restorer.

1

ASHLEY

Ashley stood at the front door knocking. She could hear a baby's cries. No one answered. She knocked again. Still no answer. There was a window to the left of the door. She squinted to look through the dirty glass, but darkness answered her. She knocked again, harder this time. The wail of a baby grew louder. She needed to get inside. She pulled out her phone and dialed 911.

The fall air chilled her so she rubbed her hands together to warm them. She thought of the baby. What if it was cold too? She eyed the large hole in the screen door that sagged open. The paint on the siding was peeling off. A step was missing from the porch. The whole house seemed to groan from neglect. If this is how the house looked, what condition might the baby be in? Pound, pound, pound. She couldn't do further harm to the door if she used a bit more force.

"Stop." A child's voice rang out. She felt a tremor inside. More children? Even in the cold air, she felt sweat building under her collar as her concern escalated. She glanced at her watch as she paced. Where were the police? What was taking so long? Just then, the squad car pulled up. Relief swept over her like leaves skittering across the sidewalk from the early fall breeze.

"What's the problem ma'am?"

She flashed her identification and introduced herself. "Ashley Anderson with Child Protective Services. I received a child welfare report on this home. I can hear children, but no one is answering."

The officer stepped up to the door and pounded with his fist. "Police". The whole neighborhood should have heard that. Terrified wails came from inside. The officer tried to turn the door knob. "Guess we'll have to use force."

She nodded. The knot in her stomach tightened. Would they find no adults at all? Or a shotgun pointed in their faces?

The officer motioned her to stand back. He leaned his shoulder against the door and gave it a hard shove. It flew open with more ease than she expected. "Wait here."

Her heart pounded as she waited. A wail broke the air. The officer's shout followed. "All clear. Miss Anderson. You need to see this."

She stepped over the threshold. In the dim light, she stumbled over something. She managed to stay on her feet and kept moving toward the sound of the officer's voice. "Hey little guy. Come here. You're okay."

In the kitchen, three children huddled on the floor around an open bag of dog food. One couldn't have been more than a few months old. The older children's eyes were as big as saucers. Their mouths were covered with brown crumbs. An empty baby bottle had drained on the floor, the nipple sitting in a pool of liquid. Where were their parents? What kind of people left their children home alone? And dog food? What were these people thinking?

Adrenaline coursed through Ashley. "We need to get these children out of here! Can you help me get them to my car?" Her jaw tightened as she gathered the crying baby into her arms. The officer took the hands of the two older children and followed Ashley out the door. One by one she secured them in car seats. It was a tight fit, but her sedan could accommodate three child seats.

Once the children were secured, she turned to the officer. "Thank you so much."

"You take care of these little ones and that will be thanks enough."

"I will. They are the reason I do what I do."

"Same for me ma'am." He tipped his hat. "I'll file a police report. Is there anything else I can do?"

She nodded and pulled out her business card. After scribbling a message on the back, she handed it to him. "Could you please put this on the door?"

He took her card and attached it to a crevice in the door. While he did that, she retrieved snacks and a couple boxes of juice from the food pack kept in her car. When she handed them to the older children, dirt-stained hands reached out and took what she offered. The baby had fallen asleep. She hoped he'd remain that way until she could get back to the office. She could get formula and a clean bottle there.

As she pulled away from the curb, she waved to the officer. In the rearview mirror, she caught the oldest child's eyes. They were wide with fear. Tears left clean trails down his dusty cheeks, but he made no sound. Her eyes stung. These poor children. Then she thought of the parents. Her hands tightened around the steering wheel and a familiar knot tugged in her stomach. Why would people neglect or abuse their children?

At the office, she located a staff member who could attend to the children while she made calls to find a foster home. With the first call she succeeded in placing the baby. She hated to split up the siblings, but she didn't have many foster homes to call on. It took two more calls to place the older siblings together. She loaded them back into her car, delivered them to the two homes and helped them settle in. Both foster homes had taken in a number of children. She knew they were in good hands.

Back at the office, she flipped the light on and moved to sit at her desk. Her eyes landed on a family picture she received yesterday. She worked with them for two years and now they were back together. Their smiles said it all. Thank you notes from other families lined the bulletin board behind her desk.

Reaching into her leather bag, she pulled out her laptop and turned it on. She needed to open a case for the three children. She typed in the little information she had. If the adults in the home contacted her, she could fill in the rest. And when they did, she'd have a thing or two to say to them. A tired sigh escaped her.

She turned to grab a folder from the drawer behind her and banged her knee on the desk corner. Ouch. She would be glad to get that bulky filing cabinet moved out since the files were being computerized. With folder in hand, she moved back to the desk and caught sight of another manila folder. She still needed to get her supervisor's signature for that case file. Once she'd acquired that, she could scan it and close the case. She opened her top drawer, grabbed a pen and a yellow sticky note, then scribbled a reminder.

Her cell phone vibrated in her pants pocket. She pulled out the phone and noticed her mom's number. Her brow creased. Her mom never called her at work. Ashley answered. "Hi Mom. What's up?"

A long pause followed. "Honey, I need you to come to the hospital. It's your dad."

"What happened?"

"Oh honey. Just come."

"I'll be right there."

She grabbed her coat and raced out of her office. Feelings of nausea rose in her stomach. She gulped in big breaths as she tried to remain calm. In the twenty minutes it took to drive to the hospital, the possibilities of what happened seemed to multiply.

At the parking lot, she parked her car and ran toward the hospital. The electric doors to the ER seemed to be in slow motion as she strained to get through. She saw her mom sitting in a chair on the far end of the waiting room. Tears streamed down her face. When their eyes met, her mom stood and rushed to Ashley.

Ashley pulled her into a tight hug. "Mom, what's going on?"

She seemed unable to talk as she shook her head back and forth. Her hand covered her mouth.

A doctor approached with a somber expression. His eyes were soft with sadness. He extended his hand to her and introduced himself, although she didn't hear his name. Her ears would absorb only one detail. Why was she here and where was her dad?

"Please follow me. There's a place we can talk in private." The women followed in silent obedience. He pointed to a couple chairs so they sat. He turned his gaze to her. "Your father was brought in by ambulance. He had a heart attack. We did everything we could. I'm sorry, but we couldn't revive him. He is gone."

Sobs came out in gasping breaths. Clutching her mom, she cried into her shoulder. Her mom clutched her too. The doctor stood by in silence, giving them space. A short time passed. He reached out and touched her shoulder. "Would you like to see him?"

She nodded, her voice failing her. They stood to follow him down the hall. As they walked arm in arm, she could feel her mom trembling. Ashley worried her mom might collapse. She shifted her grip to her mom's waist. It felt as if she half-carried her mom as they approached a room and slowed.

The doctor stepped aside and raised his hand to indicate they should enter. A sheet covered someone on the bed. The doctor moved forward and lifted the sheet. Dad. Oh Dad. How she wished it wasn't him. Tears rolled down her face. She bit her lower lip to keep it from trembling and then moved closer. A peaceful expression rested on his face. A softness no longer held the demands and stresses of life. He no longer looked tired, but he no longer smiled either, and with that thought, she broke down into gut-wrenching sobs.

2

ASHLEY

Ashley spent the night at her parent's house, not wanting her mom to be alone. When she woke, a heaviness hung in the room. Disbelief came over her. He couldn't be gone, could he?

She pushed her feet into her slippers. As she walked down the hall toward the kitchen, her feet made soft thuds in the carpet. How empty this house now felt. Entering the kitchen, she noticed her mom sitting at the table, her head resting in her hands. When she lifted her head, her eyes were swollen. Although her mom normally dressed to the nines, today she only managed to pull on her robe. Ashley considered for a moment that she probably looked just as haggard. She bent to put her arm around her mom's shoulder and kissed her cheek. They both began to cry.

They stayed that way for a bit. Then she straightened and moved to make a pot of coffee. They both could use a cup. The room remained silent except for the steady sound of water dripping into the glass pot. When the last drop hit the hot liquid, Ashley poured a cup and set it in front of her mom.

"Thank you love." Her voice came out in a raspy whisper.

Ashley had never seen her mom like this. Her usual quiet faith gave her a strength that seemed larger than life. This morning it seemed to have evaporated. She looked like a lost child. Ashley felt lost too, but there were decisions to make. Someone needed to call her aunts, uncles, and cousins. They needed to contact the mortician and pastor. For now, in the quiet kitchen, she paused to try to absorb what must be faced. They would both have to adjust to the fact that this home no longer held the largeness of her dad.

*   *   *   *   *

Five days later, a black limousine pulled into the driveway to pick them up for the funeral. Numbing grief somehow carried them to this day. The sun hid behind dark clouds which added weight to the sadness.

An early morning shower left the ground soggy. They tip-toed around shallow puddles on the sidewalk as they made their way to the limousine. Ashley took her mom's arm. It made her feel stronger. Her mom looked at her and a slight smile crossed her face. "You look lovely, Ashley. Your dad loved that dress on you." Thinking of how Dad had given her the matching navy scarf for her birthday caused her to smile. He was such a thoughtful man.

Once they settled into the limousine, silence filled the space as Ashley stared out the window. As the limousine began to move, droplets of rain streamed across the glass. The maple trees dripped water droplets that clung from the rain. They seemed to be crying the tears she dared not let escape. She turned her focus to the brick homes they passed. They mirrored her resolve to remain solid and composed. The neighborhood seemed different today. Then again, everything seemed different without Dad.

As the limousine pulled up in front of the church, Ashley noted cars already filled the parking lot. Looking toward the building, the stone arches over the doorways seemed cold and uninviting, while the stained-glass windows appeared dull and flat. The driver opened the door, but Ashley sat for a moment. She closed her eyes and took a long calming breath. She turned to her mom. "Ready?"

A silent nod was her only response.

Ashley exited first and reached back in to take her mom's hand. They walked arm in arm. With each step toward the church, a heaviness filled Ashley's chest. She bit her lip and took another deep breath. She needed to keep her emotions in check.

People started gathering. She recognized many of them, but there were others she didn't. She realized a large circle of professional contacts from her dad's world were here. Most she hadn't met. How nice they had come to honor her father and yet, he should be the one receiving it, not her. She didn't like being the center of attention. An uncomfortable pit formed in her stomach. She felt out of place.

As she made her way into the church, she touched those who reached out. Then she sat with her mother in the front pew. The service began. All the words from the pastor and friends seemed to bounce away without her absorbing them. Finally, it ended. Then came the reception. After gracious thank yous and polite conversation, the guests left. When the day came to an end, she collapsed into bed. She hoped in the morning, she would find it all a bad dream.

3

ASHLEY

With so many cases and children to monitor, Ashley couldn't take much time off work. Parents don't stop abusing their children just because she had a family emergency. Back at work, her first priority was to check on the three children she placed in foster care the day of her dad's death. To date, no adult had contacted the department. It appeared the children were abandoned.

At their foster home, the two older children hovered close to the foster mom. A good sign. It indicated they felt safe and comfortable. What a difference it made to see them clean.

In the days that passed, she succumbed to the sea of cases that passed over her desk. It helped to be busy. Her work provided a distraction from her dad's death. Her new supervisor, Robin, created another distraction. Robin's rigid and demanding nature elevated the tension at work. Maybe it had more to do with her own grief.

A month passed since her father's funeral. Her best friend Teri insisted on getting together, claiming it would be good for her. Ashley felt like going out as much as she felt like getting a root canal. She just wasn't ready. Her dad's death felt too fresh, but they had agreed upon tonight. Ashley closed her computer for the evening and drove to their favorite Seattle wine bar. It had a cozy atmosphere where they could sit at a table for the whole night if they chose. The staff knew them, so she felt among friends.

As she pulled into the parking lot, she spotted Teri's car. Making her way inside, she glanced toward their usual corner table. Teri stood and waved to catch her attention. After a quick embrace, Teri touched her arm. "So how are you?"

Ashley knew her inquiry referred to the loss of her dad, but she found it hard to talk about him. It seemed to reignite the pain, not that it ever went away. She needed to keep the conversation light. "For a girl who worked fifty-five hours this week, I'm doing ok." Rolling her eyes, she sighed and feigned exhaustion.

"You're right about that. That's all you do. You've got to get a life!"

"They are my life!"

"I know, the kids. Good thing they have you too, but you need some kids of your own. It's time to get serious about a man."

"Oh you." She nudged Teri. "Let's get a glass of wine. Heck, what am I thinking? We better just order a bottle."

"That's my girl!" Teri laughed.

Ashley caught the waitress' eye. She ordered their favorite Riesling and shifted her attention back to Teri. "Enough about me. Let's hear about you. Any chance you're wearing a ring yet?"

"You know that's not happening right now." Teri nor her boyfriend Eric seemed to be in a hurry to tie the knot. They were content pursuing their careers and enjoying life without further commitment.

"So, why the long hours Ashley?" Teri always got right to the core of a conversation.

"It's a long list. You don't want to know." She paused and swallowed a lump in her throat. "One case has been harder. I started working on behalf of three children who were abandoned about a month ago."

"Oh my gosh. That's horrible. What will happen to them?"

Ashley felt a tightness in her throat. Since her father's death, she felt more emotional than usual. She turned her attention to the tiny lights above the bar, a nice addition to the dark wood. They made the room feel more intimate. Ashley realized she had gotten lost in thought. She cleared her throat and looked back at Teri who was still watching her, waiting for a response.

"I've found two nice foster homes. The state will proceed with getting permanent custody so I'll be looking for adoptive families. It would be nice if one family could take all three of them, but that rarely happens."

Before Teri could respond, a pair of drinks arrived instead of their wine. The waitress pointed toward a table where two men were quick to nod at them. Ashley noticed one in particular. His clean-shaven face accentuated his short dark hair. He wore a dress shirt and blue-striped tie. A suit jacket hung over the back of his chair. Ashley felt a flutter in her chest when their eyes met. She nodded her thanks and looked away. As intriguing as he appeared, she didn't need a relationship. Between work and her mom, who needed her now more than ever, life overflowed with too much already. Without intending to, she glanced again at their table. His dark brown eyes were locked on her. She turned away again and forced herself back into the conversation with Teri.

Teri shared news of her mom's upcoming retirement party, but Ashley's mind strayed to the handsome man at the corner table. Before long, Teri raised an eyebrow and nudged Ashley under the table. "Don't tell me you haven't noticed."

Ashley could feel her face flush. "Yes Teri, but seriously! You know my life. Besides, I highly doubt he's interested."

"That's not how it looks to me. He looks plenty interested! And who can blame him? You are drop-dead gorgeous. Those baby blues of yours..."

"Oh stop! Besides, even if he is, I'm enjoying my time with you. Besides, I think we've already been over this. Who would want a relationship with someone who does nothing but work?" Her words sounded flat and meaningless. Her own resolve seemed to be evaporating.

"It doesn't have to be that way."

She glanced at the man again. Their eyes met. She diverted her glance in an effort to pretend she hadn't seen him. With a tinge of regret, she stood to leave. "Teri, I'm exhausted. I appreciate you meeting with me tonight."

Teri stood to hug her as she gathered her own coat. "I'll walk out with you. I'm tired too, but I'm glad it worked out to get together." She hesitated and nodded toward the table with the men. "Are you sure you don't want to introduce yourself?"

Ashley smiled and winked. "Let's go." She turned toward the door, determined to avoid making eye contact with the handsome guy. He simply didn't fit into the reality of her life. At least not right now.

4

ASHLEY

Ashley continued to throw herself into work. What else could she do with the gaping hole in her heart left from her father's death? She thought of the saying, "Time helps heal all wounds." It didn't feel that way. With each passing day, the hole in her heart felt as large as the day before. She appreciated the meaningful work to keep her occupied.

Today she and her co-worker James were given another new case to investigate. Pulling up to the curb of a small house, she noticed disrepair. The wooden stairs to the porch sagged. A skinny cat lay stretched across the step. She stepped over it. When she reached to ring the doorbell, she noticed it hanging by an exposed electrical wire. She decided to just knock.

A man in a sleeveless t-shirt and dirty jeans answered the door.

"Mr. Acer?"

"Who wants to know?"

"We're from Child Protective Services. We've received a call to do a welfare check since the children haven't been in school the last three days. May we come in?"

The man glowered over them and then stepped aside, allowing them to enter. The house reeked of cat urine. She struggled to keep from covering her nose.

"Mr. Acer, we would like to see your children."

"They're sick." The gruffness in his voice sent a chill down Ashley's spine.

"May we see them?" Her voice sounded more confident than she felt.

He remained silent, seeming to weigh his options. Time seemed to drag.

"Mr. Acer?"

Without a word, he turned and started down a narrow hall, the carpet was worn to bare wood. They followed him. As he opened the door to a bedroom, the smell of vomit made her cough. Inside were the two children, covered in their own excrement.

She saw a garbage can, grabbed it, and lost her lunch in it. She felt light-headed, but needed to keep her senses about her. She couldn't leave these children like this.

James stepped forward. "Mr. Acer, it appears your children are in need of medical care. We are going to take them to a clinic right away."

Acer seemed unconcerned. "Do whatever you want. I'm tired of taking care of them. Since their mama ran off, they're always sick. You take them."

She didn't need any further encouragement. She gathered the little girl into her arms and James lifted the little boy. Her stomach lurched and her head swirled. She couldn't take another round of embarrassment by vomiting again, so she did her best to hold her breath.

As they stepped outside, she gasped in big gulps of fresh air. Taking quick steps, she reached the car and leaned against it, still holding the little girl. James buckled the boy into the back seat and then retrieved the girl from Ashley's arms. Ashley sunk into the front seat and leaned her head on the cool dashboard. The stench from the home followed them to the car. She unrolled the window and drew in more breaths.

James took his place in the driver's seat. "Hey, are you okay?"

Ashley nodded. She dared not open her mouth to speak. She glanced back at the house. Mr. Acer stood on the porch. His arms were crossed across his chest and a cigarette drooped from his lips. Ashley shook her head in disbelief. She had seen her share of neglectful situations. This was among the worst. The Acer children were safe now. Before the day ended, they would receive proper medical care, a foster home, and a bath. If she had her way about it, Mr. Acer would never parent them again.

As they pulled away from the curb, Ashley thought of the stark contrast to her own father. Why would a father like Acer be allowed to live while her own wonderful father died so young?

5

ASHLEY

The weekend had arrived. Ashley promised to help her mom go through some of her dad's personal belongings. It was time. It was also time for another conversation. She hoped she could bring up the subject of her adoption. Since the passing of her dad, she had a fresh curiosity about her past. Her mom might be the only one with answers. She felt a new urgency to learn more.

Arriving at her mom's house, she let herself in and called out. "Mom, I'm here. Where are you?"

Her mom rushed out from the kitchen to greet her at the door. "Oh Ashley, thanks so much for coming today."

"Of course." She glanced at her dad's leather recliner. A book rested on the coffee table next to it. A bookmark indicated where he stopped reading, a reminder of another thing left unfinished. She fought an urge to grab a blanket and curl up in the chair as she had done so many times in her younger years with her dad.

Her mom caught her by the hand and led her into the kitchen where warm cookies were cooling. Snitching one off the cookie sheet, she sat at the table and chatted about the week, trying to delay the task ahead. After about twenty minutes, the conversation lulled. Their eyes met. Without saying a word, her mom rose and started toward her bedroom. Ashley followed.

This home contained good memories. Entering the hall, she noticed the dozens of family pictures lining the wall. Her high school and college graduation pictures were among them. She paused to look at one where she and her dad posed with Mickey Mouse. She was only eight at the time, but she could still remember. Making her way down the hall, she allowed her finger to trail against the texture of the wall, just as she had done as a little girl. It made her think of happier days when they weren't faced with the difficult task of today.

Ashley entered their bedroom. The burgundy brocade bedspread covered the bed with matching pillow shams fluffed and positioned at the top of the bed. The overstuffed chair looked odd without her mom sitting in it. Growing up, Ashley often found her mom there in the early morning hours studying her Bible.

Ashley moved to the walk-in closet. Her mom removed business shirts and suits from the hangers. Ashley joined her. As she slid a shirt off its hanger, the smell of her dad's cologne caught her by surprise. Tears welled in her eyes. Gulping, she swallowed hard. There was too much to do for her to be melting into tears.

She cleared her throat and plunged into her question. "Mom, I've been thinking about my adoption. I wonder..." She paused, taking a deep breath as she pinched her lips between her teeth. She no longer seemed certain how or what to ask.

"What honey? What are you wondering about?"

She took another deep breath. "A lot of things. I wonder why I was put up for adoption. I wonder if being adopted had an influence on my decision to become a caseworker." She paused, noticing how crisp each of her dad's shirts were. As an attorney, he was a man of order as evidenced by his shoes, lined up in a neat row, polished and ready to wear.

Her mom smiled. "It could have, but honey, I think you were born to be one. You've had a tender heart for as long as I can remember. You made new children at school feel welcome, sitting with them at the lunchroom table. You looked after that sweet girl who used a wheelchair."

It had been a long time since she'd thought of those friends. It made her smile at the memories. She wondered what happened to them. She pressed on. "Mom, tell me my story. I was so young. I don't remember any of it. As far as I recall, you and Dad have always been my parents."

Her mom sat down on the edge of the bed, still holding a white shirt. "We always wanted children. When we learned I couldn't have them, we were devastated."

Ashley nodded as she folded a shirt.

"Your dad suggested we become foster parents. In his years as an attorney, he had seen many children in need, but I was resistant. As a teacher, I'd also taught foster children. Many of them had behavioral issues. Some seemed vacant and lost. It was one thing being their teacher, but I wondered if I could be their mother."

"Yes, and I remember going in after school to help you. I decorated your bulletin boards while you worked with a child who needed extra help. You were so patient with them."

Her mom reached to give her hand a little squeeze. "That is so kind of you to remember. I loved teaching."

"You were a great teacher, Mom." She took a deep breath. "So, what made you change your mind?"

"You did."

The shirt Ashley had just pulled from a hanger slipped to the floor. Without leaning to pick it up, she tipped her head to the side and frowned. "I don't think I understand."

"Your dad called one day to say a three-year-old girl needed a foster home. The moment he said that, I couldn't say no. So, you arrived at our house and we immediately fell in love with you. By the grace of God, you came up for adoption. You were the answer to our prayers."

Ashley heard pieces of this story before, but it seemed more important to remember the details now.

"After you came into our lives, I saw foster children in a new light. I kept thinking one of them could have been you. My heart ached for those children that didn't get a permanent home. Often, they were only with us a few months and then they would be gone, off to a new foster home. I always wondered what happened to them." Her voice trailed off.

Ashley noticed the drapery fluttering. She moved to the window and looked out. A dark cloud caused mid-day to look like evening. A storm must be moving in. As she leaned toward the window to shut it, she caught a whiff of the sweet pea blossoms right outside. She closed her eyes and inhaled. It smelled like home.

"Thanks for shutting that honey."

Ashley opened her eyes and moved back to the closet. She pulled a few ties from the tie rack. She needed to continue the conversation. "So, in all reality Mom, my passion to be a caseworker may have come from you."

Her mom smiled. "As much as I'd like to take credit, I think it's a part of your DNA."

Ashley let out a breath she didn't realize she'd been holding. "My DNA. Mom." She licked her lips. They felt dry. She needed a drink of water, but didn't want to break the conversation. "Do you know anything about my biological family? Or anything about my life before I came to you and Dad?"

Her mom paused, inhaled and then exhaled a soft slow breath. "No, I really don't but I've often wondered if you remember anything. Even though you were so little, your work as a caseworker might trigger memories from your past. Has that ever happened?"

She thought of the reoccurring dream that seemed to have followed her into her adulthood. Perhaps it was a memory, but now didn't seem like the best time to mention it, their grief still too fresh. She ran her fingers through her hair.

"No, I can't remember anything. Maybe that's good. From what I see, people who lose their children aren't very good parents. I know having you and Dad was the best thing that could have happened for me. I am one of the lucky ones. I am curious though."

"I'm sure you are. I am too, but it wasn't luck honey. It was God's providence." It was so like her mom to refer to God and give him credit. Her faith oozed from her life. "Our lives became whole once you were a part of it. It wasn't easy though. I remember how you used to cry yourself to sleep. I would rock you and rub your back, but you seemed lost in some sad place. It broke my heart. In time, your night-time tears evaporated. You must have sensed you were safe and loved."

Ashley didn't remember that. For a moment she took it in. She glanced at her mom. She fingered the cross around her neck. Ashley regretted bringing up her adoption and realized she needed to lighten the moment. "Mom, I only remember my time with you and Dad. You let me finger paint on the most random things. Do you remember when you let me paint the refrigerator doors? You made me feel like I'd created a masterpiece. How long did the refrigerator stay that way?"

Her mom smiled, one of her first genuine smiles since Dad's death. "Not long enough. Where did the time go? Those were such simple, special times." She paused. "I regret I don't have any baby pictures of you."

Ashley nodded. "That would have been nice Mom, but you made sure there were lots of pictures through the years; and lots of memories to go with them. I loved our trips to Disneyland and Hawaii. How many kids get to go to places like Hong Kong and Thailand? You and Dad filled my life with magic."

Her mom reached to squeeze her hand. "We did have fun, didn't we?"

"Yes, but you know what I loved most?"

"What honey?" She raised her eyebrows.

"How you were always there for me. You sat on those hard folding chairs during every piano recital, clapping as if I performed like Beethoven."

Her mom let out a playful groan. "Those were hard chairs."

"I remember looking into the stands during gymnastic meets and seeing you smile and wave. You practically wore a path into the tiles at swim meets as you cheered me along from the side of the pool." Ashley mimicked her mom's actions, pacing with intensity from one side of the closet to the other.

Her mom smirked. "How could I help myself? You were always amazing."

She gave her mom a hug. "You might be biased Mom." They shared a smile. "Thank you. I'm not sure I thanked you enough. I always knew you were there for me."

Her mom reached to touch Ashley's cheek with the palm of her hand.

"Mom, I appreciate how you taught me to love life and to enjoy the small things; like cooking or a quiet evening playing a board game."

"I only wish your dad could have joined us more often." Her mom's hand fell to her side.

"Me too, but I understand why he put so many hours in at the office." Ashley felt like she needed to defend her dad.

Her mom nodded and smiled. "He wanted the best for the three of us."

"And he gave it to us."

Her mom reached to touch Ashley's cheek again. "I am so glad we have each other. I don't know what I would do without you, especially now."

Tears filled her eyes and a lump formed in her throat. "Oh Mom, how will we ever make it without Dad?" She pulled her mom into a tight hug as the ache of missing her dad intensified. Her mind thrashed between thoughts of her dad and curiosity of her biological family. Why did she feel such a draw to learn more about her biological family now that her dad was gone?

6

SARAH

As the Saturday morning sun stretched a warm beam across Sarah's face, her eyes fluttered open. Her husband Tyler leaned on one elbow as he watched her. She smiled as she noticed his hair. It stood up in erratic shoots. His unshaken face made his brown eyes seem darker.

"Good morning," he whispered. His finger reached to tuck a strand of her light brown hair around her ear.

"Good morning to you." She lifted her head to steal a kiss.

"How about we stay here a little longer?" He nuzzled close and pulled her into his arms.

She looked at the bedside clock. Seven-thirty. She groaned. "The kids will be awake soon. I need to get breakfast on." Twisting herself free, she scurried to the bathroom. She smiled when she saw him fall back on the pillow, feigning a pout. In the bathroom, she took a moment to brush her teeth and put on her baggy but comfortable gray sweats.

When she opened the bathroom door and stepped into the bedroom, Tyler let out a groan. "Wow, talk about killing the moment."

"Oh you." She leaned over and gave him a long, slow kiss. He reached to pull her down. She giggled, squirmed away and made a beeline for the bedroom door. Just as she reached the door, he called out, "It looks like it's going to be a beautiful day. How about going to the pool?"

"Sounds like fun." She paused to consider. "I better not though. I'd planned to get the laundry caught up today. I am so behind after picking up those extra shifts this week. You should go and take the kids. They would love a day with JUST YOU."

"Are you sure? You're pretty hot in a swimming suit."

"I'm sure." She felt her cheeks get warm. After all these years, he could still make her blush. "Go and enjoy the day with the kids. I'll get a few things done at home. Then tonight..." She let her words hang in the air. "I'll leave that to your imagination." She headed for the kitchen.

Flipping on the kitchen light, she noticed dirty dishes stacked on the counter. She let out a tired sigh. After her long day at work, she hadn't bothered to wash the dishes last night, another task needing to be done. She opened the refrigerator and inhaled a sour smell. Grabbing the milk container, she gave it a whiff. Yuck. She poured the sour milk down the sink. The whole refrigerator could use a good cleaning. To think laundry was the only thing she thought needed to be caught up today.

She located the skillet at the bottom of the stack of dirty dishes and washed it out. Grabbing the bacon from the back of the refrigerator, she pulled the sticky pieces apart and arranged them on the skillet. They began to sizzle and pop, sending a tantalizing aroma into the air.

Soon, her three groggy darlings came stumbling into the kitchen. Eighteen-month-old Noah must have climbed out of his crib again as he stood sucking his thumb with his blankie in hand. Seeing him reminded Sarah it might be time to move him to a toddler bed. Her baby was growing up too fast.

Seven-year-old Ryan spoke first. "Mom, that sure smells good."

"Sure does," little sister Leanna chimed in.

"Suh du," Noah mimicked his big sister.

Tyler soon joined them, fresh from the shower. As he came up behind her, he put his arms around her waist.

"I'm busy here," she warned.

"Get a room," Ryan added.

Sarah gave Tyler an accusatory glare. "Where did he hear that?"

Tyler shook his head and leaned to grab Ryan, wrestling him to the floor. Leanna soon joined the dog pile and their laughter bounced across the room. They were delighted to have their father's attention.

After they were all seated at the table, Tyler cleared his throat and spoke with a serious tone. "I have an announcement to make." The children's eyes widened as they looked at one another and then turned their attention to their daddy.

"Any child who eats their whole breakfast may go to the swimming pool with me today."

Ryan bounced up and down in his chair. Leanna slid off her chair and ran over to give her dad a hug around the neck. "Yes, Daddy, yes. Let's go."

"Now hold on. I said after breakfast." Both children were back in their seat, but couldn't contain their wiggles as they gobbled down their breakfast. With the last bite still being chewed, the two older children sprinted to their rooms and came back in their swimming suits. Leanna only had one arm in her swimsuit so Sarah assisted her. She grabbed a swimming diaper and trunks and dressed Noah. While they jostled, she attempted to rub sunscreen onto their exposed skin.

After gathering the beach towels, life jackets, and floating toys, they scurried to the car. At the last minute, Sarah ran back into the house to retrieve the camera. She handed it to Tyler. "Please try to get a few pictures. You know how I love pictures of the kids playing."

"I'll take some Mom." Ryan loved taking pictures.

"That would be wonderful. Ask Dad first so we don't waste film."

His dad winked at Ryan and he grinned.

With that, they loaded into the car. Huge smiles were plastered across their faces as they waved from the backseat window.

Sarah waved back, blowing them kisses. Their giggles lingered in the driveway. She paused, taking in the smells of the summer; fresh cut grass, the charcoal of a barbeque somewhere, the flowering trees. She made her way up the front steps and noticed the flower bed needed to be weeded. She loved summer in Seattle, but summer brought additional outside chores. Ryan could help. She would give him that task when they got back from the pool.

Sarah hated missing out on the fun with her family, but if she didn't attend to chores at home, it would make for a rough start to the week. As she hustled around the house, doing the laundry, mopping and vacuuming, time flew. When she heard the car pull into the garage, it surprised her to think they were back already. Glancing at the clock, she realized they had been gone over three hours. They would be hungry.

She greeted them at the front door as the children came tumbling in. Ryan sounded breathless. "Oh Mama, you won't believe what Daddy did. He let us take turns jumping off the diving board."

She paled at the thought. Although Ryan believed himself to be quite grown up at seven, Leanna was only two and a half. Granted, she acted half fish around the water, but what had Tyler been thinking?

Ryan rambled on; his voice high-pitched with excitement as the family moved toward the kitchen. "Mommy, it was so much fun. And I caught Noah when he fell in."

Sarah gasped as her hand flew to cover her mouth. "What do you mean, he fell in? Didn't he have his lifejacket on?" She reached for Noah and sat on a kitchen chair, pulling him onto her lap. She looked him over as she searched for any injuries, but he looked fine. His sweet grin made her realize she was being a worry wart. His only issue was the wet diaper that now soaked into her pants.

25

Ryan continued with his story. "Yes Mom, his face went under just a bit, but I saved him." Ryan puffed out his chest and raised clenched fists in the air like a superhero.

She smiled at him. "Oh son, you are such a big boy. Thank you for looking out for Noah." She leaned to give him a kiss on the cheek.

"Mom..." He pulled away. "I'm too big for kisses."

She ruffled his hair. "You'll never be too big, my son."

Leanna tugged on Sarah's shirt. "Yes Leanna, what do you want to tell me?"

"Daddy got ice cream."

Oh yes, the brown smudges on their towels and t-shirts were a dead giveaway for chocolate ice cream. Sarah's eyebrows raised as she cast an accusing stare at Tyler. "So, you're the one responsible for ruining their appetite?" This wasn't the first time he'd been guilty of this deed.

"What's a swimming day without ice cream?" He pulled her into his arms. "We missed you by the way."

"Ya, I bet. You wouldn't have gotten away with your shenanigans if I'd have been along. You must be hungry for lunch. Ryan and Leanna, go get dry clothes on while I change Noah." She picked up Noah and carried him to his room. He rubbed his eyes and yawned while she changed him. With dry clothes, she lifted him and he laid his head on her shoulder. He must be more tired than hungry, so she put him in his crib and stooped to kiss his damp hair. He could nap while she fixed lunch. As she stepped away from the crib, he coughed a few times. She furrowed her brow. I hope he isn't catching a cold. She glanced at him again, his long lashes already shut over his eyes. Nothing looked sweeter than a sleeping child.

Back in the kitchen, Ryan had changed into clean, dry clothes and Leanna struggled to get her shirt on. She could almost dress herself. "Mom, can we watch a movie?"

"That's a great idea." That would give her time to get lunch ready. "How does Jungle Book sound?"

They nodded their affirmation. She grabbed the tape, popped it into the VHS player, and hit Play. With the children settled on the couch, she started for the kitchen. When she opened the refrigerator to grab the milk, she remembered pouring it down the sink. She groaned. She would need some for lunch. "Tyler," she called from the kitchen, "I need to run to the store to get milk for mac and cheese. I'll be right back."

Pulling out of their driveway, she noticed her neighbors George and April. They were sitting on their front porch, sipping a glass of refreshment. She gave them a wave and continued toward the store. Her thoughts drifted to how much she loved summer. It brought her neighbors outside more often and gave them opportunities to catch up with one another. Perhaps one of these weekends she could enjoy some quiet time on their porch too.

Thirty minutes later, Sarah returned. When she made the turn onto their street, she gasped. The flashing lights of a fire truck lit up the neighborhood. Then she noticed an ambulance parked in front of her house! Her heart pounded hard in her chest as her sweaty hands tightened on the steering wheel. Negotiating the final turn, she accelerated and pulled up next to the ambulance. The car lurched to a sudden stop when she slammed on the brakes. She jumped out and ran up the sidewalk, leaving the car door gaping open.

Ryan stood on the top step. Tears streamed down his pale face.

"What happened?"

"It's Noah. Daddy can't wake him."

Dragging Ryan by the hand, she sprinted into the house. Once inside, she saw EMTs giving Noah CPR.

"No, no! What happened?" She felt woozy as the room started to spin.

Tyler knelt on the floor beside Noah. When she cried out, Tyler stood and rushed to her side, wrapping his arms around her. Sarah felt her body tremble in his arms.

One of the EMTs looked up. "We'll meet you at the hospital." They loaded Noah onto a gurney as one of the EMTs continued CPR. They wheeled the gurney toward the ambulance. Sarah and Tyler followed while Ryan and Leanna followed behind.

Once outside, Sarah noticed George and April rushing across the street toward them. "Can we help?"

"Yes. Can you stay with Ryan and Leanna?"

"Of course. Go."

"I haven't fed them lunch."

"It's okay. We'll take care of it." April leaned to put her arms around the children.

Sarah turned to Ryan and Leanna. "Mind Miss April." The children nodded in quiet obedience with their eyes as big as saucers.

As the ambulance pulled away from the house, Tyler rushed to the car and started the ignition. Sarah scurried to the passenger side and Tyler slammed the car into gear. At first, she could see the ambulance a block ahead of them, but when they were delayed by a traffic light, she lost sight of it.

At the hospital, Tyler screeched the car to a stop. He leaped out and ran around to her side of the car, grabbed her hand, and together they ran toward the ER entrance.

A nurse looked up as they rushed through the door.

"Our son came here by ambulance. Can you tell us where he is?" Tyler's voice strained with worry.

"Yes, please follow me." The nurse led them to a hallway filled with activity and pointed toward a couch. "Please wait here." She returned to her place behind the tall desk.

Sarah could see a flurry of white coats and blue scrubs in a glass room across the hall. Then someone abruptly pulled the curtain across the glass. She couldn't see Noah. She couldn't see anything.

She jumped up and hustled to the reception desk. "Can we see him? Can we see our son?"

"The doctors are working on him. It is best you wait here."

Out of the corner of her eye, she noticed a doctor approaching. Turning toward him, she searched his face. His brows were furrowed behind thick glasses.

"Mr. and Mrs. Thornton?"

She grabbed Tyler's hand and nodded.

"The EMTs worked on your son the whole way here. We've tried everything. We haven't been able to restore a heartbeat. I'm sorry. Your son didn't make it."

7

TYLER

The days that followed were a blur. Tyler held his trembling wife as they purchased a child-sized coffin and planned a funeral for his little buddy. Sarah couldn't speak without crying so he made the painful calls to inform relatives and answered the door to neighbors who brought food. Late in the afternoon on the third day following Noah's death, the doorbell rang again. Tyler opened the door, expecting to receive another casserole but instead, there were two police officers.

"Mr. Thornton?" The taller thin officer showed his badge.

"Yes, how can I help you?" Tyler rubbed his frowning forehead.

"May we come in?"

"Um, sure, but why are you here?" He felt a tightening in his chest.

The second officer wore a thick mustache. "Sir, we just need a few moments."

Tyler stepped aside and motioned toward the living room. Sarah looked up and her face contorted as she tried to keep from crying. She snuggled with Leanna in the wooden rocking chair, reading stories. The book they were reading slid to the floor. Ryan continued to play with his GI Joe figures on the orange shag rug while keeping an eye on the police officers.

Tyler motioned toward a chair. "Would you like to sit?"

The taller officer stepped forward and cleared his throat. "No, we won't be long. We just need to ask some questions about the day your son died."

Tyler remained standing as he glanced at Sarah and then at the children. "I don't know what more I can say." He took in a ragged breath as he struggled to maintain his composure. "Noah was fine after we spent the morning at the pool. He was sleepy when we got home so Sarah laid him down for a nap. When I passed his room, I looked in on him." Tyler paused as if gathering courage to continue. His next words came out in halted gasps. He...wasn't...breathing."

The shorter officer took notes on a pad. He paused a moment to write in his pad and then turned his attention back to Tyler. "Can you tell us anything more?"

Tyler shook his head. His body shuddered at the memory. After a long pause, he gathered himself. "Have the autopsy results come back yet?"

The taller officer shifted from one foot to the other. A muscle in his jaw tightened. "No, but we need to do a little preliminary investigation while we wait."

Tyler caught his breath. His voice raised a pitch. "Investigation? What is there to investigate?"

"We just need to clarify a few details." With that, the taller police officer turned to Sarah. "Ma'am, is that how you remember it?"

Tyler could feel heat coming into his face. He knew Sarah couldn't take anymore. He stepped between the policeman and his wife. "Listen, we have to bury our son tomorrow. My wife doesn't need this right now. Can't this wait?"

The taller officer shifted his eyes between Sarah and Tyler and rested them on Tyler, giving him an extra stare. The shorter officer snapped his notebook shut and put the pencil in his shirt pocket. "Sorry to have bothered you. We will come back at another time."

Tyler escorted them to the door and shut it behind them. He rushed back to his family. Tears were rolling down Sarah's cheeks as Leanna patted her face. "Mommy, ok?" Ryan rested his hand on his mother's shoulder. His chin quivered.

Tyler pulled all three of them into his arms.

"Oh Tyler. What in the world was that about?" Sarah's eyes were wide with fear.

"I don't know." His tongue felt stuck to the roof of his mouth. He swallowed to moisten his throat and sat down on the couch, trying to stop his shaking knees. Running his fingers through his hair, he took a deep breath. "I'm sure there is nothing to worry about Sarah. They are just doing their job. This will all be behind us soon." In the back of his mind, he couldn't let go of a nagging thought. Why were the police conducting an investigation?

8

SARAH

The following day, a soft rain fell as they laid little Noah to rest. Feeling as if in a trance, Sarah greeted family and friends who joined them at the church. Ryan and Leanna clung to her and Tyler.

It was a simple service with an open casket. When it ended and the last of the guests filed out, she approached the tiny coffin and with shaking hands, tucked Noah's slightly soiled blue blankie beside him. She touched his curly hair and bent to kiss his cheek one last time. It didn't seem real.

After a short graveside service, guests and family gathered at the house and offered condolences. Sarah sat on the floral couch and willed for the house to empty. She felt completely drained. When Tyler escorted the last guest out, Sarah put her head back and closed her eyes. Moments later, another knock on the door caused her to jump. Her nerves were raw. Tyler stood to answer it. When he swung the door open, she could see the police standing on the step. Why were they here again?

Tyler's voice sounded flat with weariness as he greeted them. "I'm sorry. Whatever you need can wait."

The tall officer from the day before stepped forward. "Actually, it won't. We are here to place you under arrest for negligent homicide." His voice sounded firm and demanding.

Sarah gasped and jumped to her feet. Had she heard right? Tyler, being arrested? When she reached the door, she gripped the officer's arm. "Why are you arresting my husband?"

"I'm sorry ma'am." He offered no further explanation as he pulled his arm from her hand.

Tyler glanced from one officer to the other in disbelief. "What are you talking about?"

"I'm sorry Mr. Thornton, we've been instructed to arrest you. Please put your hands behind your back." He began to read Tyler his rights.

Sarah felt like her head was spinning. She grabbed at Tyler's shirt. "What should I do?"

His eyes were wide as he shook his head back and forth. "I don't know. I don't know."

The taller officer escorted Tyler to the squad car as the other officer hustled ahead to open the back door. Sarah followed close behind. She bit down on her bottom lip and winced. She tasted blood. She heard a distant siren and looked to see if any neighbors were around. She needed help and had no idea where to turn. She noticed a sedan and two more officers talking with a woman standing near it. They caught Sarah's eye and approached her.

The woman cleared her throat. "Mrs. Thornton, I'm with Child Protective Services. We need to take your children into our care until we can sort things out."

"What? No!" She backed away as she pushed her hands out in front of her. "No, you're not taking my children anywhere." She glared at the heavy-set woman.

"Mommy, I'm scared." Sarah turned to find Ryan at her side. "Where are they taking Daddy?" Leanna tugged on her skirt. She reached to grasp their hands and pushed the children behind her, forcing her body rigid as if becoming armor to protect her children from the woman. She glanced back at the street long enough to see the patrol car pull away from the curb with Tyler in the backseat.

Out of the corner of her eye, she could see the woman moving in closer. Sarah directed her eyes back to the woman. Sarah's eyes were filled with rage. "You are not taking my children." So focused on Tyler, the children, and the woman, Sarah hadn't noticed the policemen behind her, standing next to the children. He stepped into her line of sight. "Please don't fight this Mrs. Thornton. This is for the benefit of the children. We will get this all sorted out once they are questioned."

"Questioned? About what?" Her voice elevated to a screech. The grip she had on her children's hands tightened like a tourniquet. The policeman reached down to put an arm around Ryan. Ryan tried to squirm away, but the officer already had a grip on him and lifted him up. The woman swept in with remarkable speed for a woman her size and gathered Leanna into her arms. Sarah still had a firm grasp on each of her children. "You're not taking them!"

The officer gave her a stern look. "Ma'am. I don't want to arrest you, but if you don't cooperate, I will. Now LET GO." His demanding bark caused her to release the children.

Sarah's whole body shook as she followed them, watching as her children were being half-dragged, half-carried away, their arms stretched out toward her. Ryan kicked and clawed. "Let me go. Leave me alone. Mom, HELP!" The more he struggled, the more escalated Leanna's cries became as she too strained to break free. With Ryan in hand and Leanna hoisted in the woman's arms, they were placed in the backseat of the CPS worker's car.

It wasn't until then Sarah realized a police officer restrained her. She attempted to break free and reach her children, but she couldn't. Horror came over her when she saw her children's frantic, tear-streaked faces pressed against the window. She remembered seeing the taillights of the car disappear around the corner. Then everything went dark!

9

SARAH

Sarah could smell the sterile smells of a hospital before she even opened her eyes. She felt disoriented and confused. When her eyes fluttered open, her mom came into sight. Her eyes were red and puffy.

"What's going on? Why am I here?"

Her mom put her warm hand on Sarah's forehead. "It's good to see you awake." Her voice came out slow and sad.

Sarah reached toward a pain on her head, but an IV restricted her hand. She raised her other hand to rub her head. "Ow!" She felt a bump. "How did I get that?"

"You passed out last night and hit your head pretty hard. We've been waiting for you to wake up." Her mom's eyes filled with tears.

Sarah looked down at the stiff white gown with tiny blue dots. She felt exposed. She reached to pull a blanket up to cover herself. "How long have I been here?"

"About twelve hours."

She looked around the room. "Where's Tyler?"

Her mom took her hand in hers and rubbed it without speaking. She avoided making eye contact.

"Mom, what's going on?"

"You need to rest. You've been under a lot of stress." She eased Sarah's shoulders back down to the bed.

"Mom, you're worrying me. Please tell me what's going on."

Her mom paused as if not sure what to say. She dabbed a tissue to her eye and cleared her throat. Her words came out in a whispered rasp. "Honey, don't you remember? Noah? Tyler? The children?"

Sarah thought for a moment. "Mom, I don't know what you're talking about. In fact, why are you even here?"

Her mom's chin began to tremble as she took Sarah's hand in hers and patted it. "You've been through a lot honey. Your mind and body need rest. We are doing everything we can to help the situation."

"MOM! What's going on?"

A nurse poked her head in the door. "It's good to see you are awake."

Sarah turned her attention to the nurse. "Can you tell me what's going on?"

"First things first. How are you feeling?" The nurse began smoothing the blanket. "Are you warm enough? I could get you another warm blanket if you'd like."

"I'm fine, but I am a bit confused and I'm starting to worry. Why isn't Tyler here? Who is looking after the children?"

The nurse's eyes met her mom's and a look of concern passed between them. Then she looked back at Sarah. "That's all being taken care of. For now, the main thing is to get you back on your feet. You took a pretty nasty fall, but we've done a scan and everything is okay. You've suffered a concussion though so the doctor would like you to remain in the hospital a few days for observation."

"What? I can't stay here." She could feel her heart racing as a sticky sweat started to collect on her skin.

The nurse seemed to have noticed too. "I'm going to give you a little medicine to help you relax."

Before she could object, the nurse injected a liquid into the IV. She felt her eyes growing heavy as her body slacked in relaxation.

She looked at her mom and saw tears streaming down her face. Then sleep overcame her.

* * * * *

By the next day, the horror of the previous days slammed fully into her memory. Her eyes felt raw from tears after hashing out every detail with her parents. Sarah's dad made contact with CPS, but only Sarah could receive updates. Tyler's parents went to the jail to see Tyler. Nothing could be done until his hearing. There were no answers.

The doctor agreed to release her from the hospital around dinner time. As her parents assisted her into the car, she felt numb. Perhaps it was the medication, or perhaps it was reality assaulting every sense.

As her dad drove them to the house, the three of them were silent. Once they arrived, her parents came around the car to help her. Although she felt capable of getting herself out, her body felt like lead. Thank goodness for their assistance.

She made her way to the Formica kitchen table. She and Tyler found it at a garage sale in their earlier years. She added avocado green seat covers to help make the straight, metal chairs more comfortable. The table was wiped clean. She knew her mom must have done that because with three small children, a clean table was a rarity.

As she sat, she noticed Noah's high chair had been moved back into the corner. Her dad cleared his throat and then spoke with tenderness. "Sarah, would you like me to put that somewhere else?"

She nodded. He gathered the high chair and left the room. When he returned, he sat in the chair Ryan usually occupied, and then stared blankly across the table, his hands folded. Her mom poured coffee and served leftover lasagna. Then she moved the stack of Sears catalogs from Leanna's chair and joined them. Tyler's chair remained empty. The house felt hollow without the sounds of her children and Tyler.

Her parents ate in silence. Sarah didn't feel like eating. She pushed her food around her plate with her fork, attempting to look like she was eating. There was no point. It felt like anything she ate would come back up. She needed to see her children and Tyler, but this late in the evening, the CPS office was closed and visiting hours at the jail were over.

Her mom broke the silence. "Honey, your dad needs to go back to work. He's planning to leave tomorrow, but I can stay, if you'd like me to."

She thought for a moment. "No, I'll be fine. There is so much to do, but I'm the only one who can do it. You've already been here much longer than you anticipated. Besides, I don't want Dad driving home alone. It's a long trip. I'd feel better if you were together."

"Honey, are you sure? You've been through so much."

"I need some time. You can always come back later if I need you."

Her dad jumped in the conversation. "I'm fine driving home alone. We are most concerned with you Sarah. Are you sure Mom can't stay and help? Drive you to appointments? Help you talk through things?"

"No, I'll be fine. Once I get the kids home, I might need help until Tyler comes home, but for now, I'm fine."

Her parents looked at each other as if trying to decide what to do. Seeing their concern, she realized she'd better sound convincing if she was ever going to get them to go home. She needed time alone to think. "Dad, you'd starve to death without Mom. That's all we'd need." She tried to smile, but it felt fake. "Besides, Tyler's folks aren't as far away. If I get in a pinch, I can call on them. Once the kids are home, they'll need to get back to school and I need to return to work."

Her parents still looked uncertain.

"Really, I'll be fine. This will be over soon."

Her mom reached to squeeze her hand. "You're right honey. Everything is going to be fine."

10

SARAH

After sending her parents off early the next morning, Sarah showered, put on a clean pair of dress pants and a blouse, and drove to the CPS office. She arrived at 7:50 a.m. She wanted to talk to someone the moment the doors opened.

When she noticed an employee unlocking the front doors, she hurried to the entrance. As she entered, she noticed a large sign: "Please check in with the receptionist". She approached a desk where a maternal looking woman sat, who peered over her glasses at Sarah. "How may I help you?"

"I need to speak to a supervisor." Sarah tried to sound confident even though her knees shook.

"Your name please?"

"Sarah Thornton."

The receptionist's warm smile faded as she picked up the phone and whispered into the receiver. Within a few minutes, Sarah could hear the clicking of high heels on a hard floor. She watched as a woman in a business suit entered the waiting area. Her high heels made her a couple inches taller than Sarah. "Mrs. Thornton?"

Sarah nodded.

The woman reached out to shake Sarah's hand. "I'm Julie. Please follow me to my office where we can talk."

Sarah complied and followed in silence, feeling intimidated by the woman. As they entered a room, Sarah noticed a neat stack of folders on the desk. Documents were pinned to a bulletin board behind the desk, again in neat precision. Julie shut the door and began making her way around the desk. Sarah couldn't wait any longer. She stepped toward Julie. "Do you know where my children are?"

Julie moved behind the desk, putting some space between them. She sat and motioned with her hand toward chairs in front of her desk.

Sarah's legs felt like jelly. She sat before they could give out on her.

Julie spoke with an air of haughtiness. "They are safe Mrs. Thornton."

Sarah took a deep breath, shuddering as she exhaled. "Oh, thank God. When can I take them home?"

Julie leaned forward and put her elbows on the desk. She raised her chin. "We need to clear up a few things first, so let's not get ahead of ourselves."

Sarah gulped, trying with every ounce of her energy to restrain herself. Julie was calm to an irritable fault. Taking another breath, she tried to keep her voice steady and respectful. "Ma'am, you don't understand. My son died last week. My husband has been arrested. Now you have Ryan and Leanna. They need to be home with me."

Julie raised herself up in her chair and leaned forward on her elbows. "I DO understand Mrs. Thornton, but there is a process."

Sarah felt tears brimming at the rims of her eyes. She couldn't cry. She couldn't show any weakness. She must get her children back. She sucked in a deep breath. "Why did you take them?"

"For their protection."

Sarah grimaced and glanced around as if looking for answers. Her eyes narrowed as she looked at Julie. "Why would you think they aren't safe? None of this makes sense."

"Your son's death appears to be a result of neglect."

The word neglect rang through her head as she struggled to respond to the accusation. "Neglect? Noah wasn't neglected. He was loved. We love all our children."

"Unfortunately, that is not what his autopsy shows." Julie's response reeked of her annoying calmness.

"What do you mean?" Sarah felt panic rising inside. She took a deep breath.

"The coroner's report states your son died of secondary drowning."

"What is that? I don't understand." Sarah's stomach lurched. She felt like she might throw up as she fought to keep her tears in check. She took another deep breath. She couldn't break down. This needed to be straightened out.

Julie pushed her chair back from her desk and stood. "Mrs. Thornton. I suggest you get an attorney."

Sarah remained seated. She wasn't leaving until she had some answers. "I want my children. At least let me see them."

"I'm sorry. That won't be happening until we get a parenting plan together." Julie moved from behind her desk and stood at the door. "You'll need to make an appointment next week to visit with the caseworker who has been assigned your case."

Sarah took a deep breath and closed her eyes. When she opened them, she stood and looked at Julie. "My children must be terrified. I need to talk to them."

Julie opened the door and motioned her hand for Sarah to leave. "Mrs. Thornton. Your children are fine. They are getting the needed help. You don't need to worry about them. There's nothing more to discuss at this time."

Rage began to build inside. Sarah wanted to reach out and shake this lady. Don't worry about her children? After everything they had been through? Now they were away from home living with strangers. How could she not worry about them? Desperate for a different answer, she tried once more. "Please, may I see them? Even for a few moments? I need to reassure them everything will be okay."

"I'm sorry. There are procedures." Julie handed her a business card. "Call this caseworker and arrange a time to meet. She will have a list of requirements and a parenting plan. She'll also let you know when you can visit your children. Until then, again, I suggest you hire an attorney."

Sarah took the card with her shaking hand. She felt so angry, she needed to get out of here before she did something she might regret.

She wanted to see her children, but clearly, it wasn't going to happen today.

Walking as fast as she could, Sarah fled the office. Once she got to the safety of her car, hot tears streamed down her cheeks. She put her car in gear and headed toward the jail. She needed to see Tyler. He would know what to do.

At the jailhouse, Sarah approached the tall front desk where an officer sat above her. She had never been in a jailhouse before. She licked her lips.

The lady police officer's monotone greeting implied she had said hello a million times more than she cared.

Sarah tugged her blouse into place and cleared her throat. "I am here to see my husband."

"Name." It came out with less enthusiasm than her greeting.

"Sarah, I mean, Tyler Thornton."

"Take a seat." She pointed to a row of wood chairs; the stain worn off the arms. They reminded her of the chairs outside of her grade school principal's office, not that she spent much time in them back then.

Sarah sat on the edge of the seat. She lifted her chin to try to appear confident. Five minutes passed. Her blouse stuck to her chest and back as an uncomfortable drip made its way down the center of her back.

A policeman came through a side door. "Thornton. Follow me."

She jumped to her feet and followed closely behind. He directed her to a holding area where Tyler sat in a private cell. Bars separated them. When Tyler saw her, he stood and walked to the bars. He wore a rumpled orange jumpsuit. He looked gaunt and exhausted, his eyes bloodshot and puffy. She doubted he'd slept since he'd been arrested.

"You've got fifteen minutes." The policeman left, locking the door behind him.

Now she felt like a prisoner. She shuttered. She moved toward the cell. Tyler's hands reached out through the bars and she grabbed them. For a few moments neither could speak. Then she uttered the words she still couldn't quite believe. "Tyler, they took the kids."

An incredulous stare crossed Tyler's face and his mouth fell open. "What do you mean?"

"Child Protective Services. They took our children."

"Why?" His eyes were wide in horror.

Her throat tightened and she couldn't speak.

He pulled her as close as he could through the bars, cupped her face in his hands, and kissed her cheek. "Honey, what happened?"

She took a deep breath and told him everything as fast as she could. She knew they didn't have much time. "We need a good attorney."

His eyes were still wide as he shook his head. "I don't know one, and I'm pretty sure we can't afford one."

"Tyler, we've got to fight this!"

He nodded. "Of course." He coughed a bit as tears welled in his eyes. "I'm so sorry honey."

"It's...not...your...fault." Her words came out in jagged stutters as her body shook.

He put his finger over her lips. "Honey, we will get this figured out. I'll have my hearing. We'll get an attorney and..." She heard a squeak as the lock turned. Their time was up. She leaned in to kiss Tyler while she still could, and squeezed his hand, releasing it only when their fingers could no longer touch.

*　　*　　*　　*　　*

After Sarah left the jail, she felt ragged and exhausted. Too much to process and no clear answers. She felt all alone. Why hadn't she asked her parents to stay a little longer?

Without thought, she drove to the cemetery. She felt drawn there. It seemed like the only safe place left. When she arrived, she sat in the car, uncertain if she could face it, and yet, longing to be here. Looking out over the grassy area, she noticed a robin sitting on a nearby tree branch. Small flags yielded to a breeze. A windsock fluttered at a nearby grave.

When she got out of the car, the breeze caused her to pull her sweater closer. She could smell fresh cut grass and flowers. She paused and allowed the fragrance to fill her nostrils. She looked at her feet, willing them to move as she took halted steps toward Noah's grave.

Sod laid over what had been a hole just days ago. She stared at the fresh grave. Disbelief shadowed over her. Noah, sweet Noah. She hadn't even taken the time to grieve for her baby. With painstaking effort, she lowered herself to the ground and began sobbing. She thought she'd cried all her tears the day they buried him, but somewhere, deep in her soul, tears ripped from her heart. She began to pray. "God, I don't know what to do. I don't know who to talk to. I don't even know if you are there or if you can help me. I have nowhere else to turn. Please help me. Please tell me what I should do. Oh God, please help me get my family back."

She wasn't sure how long she sat on the ground, praying at Noah's grave, but when her tears stopped, she felt calmer. She felt a sense of peace. She knew what she needed to do next.

11

ASHLEY

Ashley glanced at her watch. Time to head to the courthouse. She gathered her file for the three children she found alone in the home with nothing to eat but dog food. Today she would testify on their behalf. She hoped she could help them move toward a permanent home soon.

She squeezed into the back row of the packed courtroom, excusing herself as she negotiated past those already sitting. It appeared she arrived well ahead of her case. As she looked toward the judge's bench, she did a double take. It was him, the guy who bought her and Teri a drink a couple months ago. She watched him. He seemed preoccupied with his cell phone, so he hadn't looked her way.

As the bailiff called for the next case, the handsome stranger went to the defense table. Ah, he must be a defense attorney. This could be interesting since she often sat on the prosecutor's side as a witness for the state. The judge addressed the man as Mr. Ellington. At least now she knew his last name.

Mr. Ellington stood with confidence and poise as he gave his opening statement. His hand gestures drew her into his comments. He spoke with well-planned pauses, giving time for his words to sink in, and his soothing voice made the room feel calm. He was easy to look at too. His navy business suit accentuated his dark hair and fair skin. His muscular shoulders were evident under the suit jacket. She felt her face flush when she realized she'd been staring.

So lost in thought, she hadn't noticed the judge called the next case forward.

She glanced down at her case number. It wouldn't be called for at least fifteen minutes. Looking up, she noticed Mr. Ellington making his way down the center aisle. Without thinking, she stood and moved toward the aisle, stumbling across a few ankles on the way. She arrived just as he got to her row. His eyes met hers. His head jerked up. He took a step back as his mouth flew open.

She stifled a giggle, but a smile couldn't be held back. Although she had no intention of starting a relationship, this created an interesting turn of events. She had to admit, she would like to meet him.

He cleared his throat and whispered. "Hi there."

"Hello." Her response came out a bit breathy. She could feel her cheeks getting hot. How embarrassing.

"Weren't you at the wine bar awhile back?" he again whispered, sounding a bit flirtatious.

She nodded yes, trying to keep their conversation to a minimum with the court in session.

 Besides, for some reason, speaking seemed to be a bit of a challenge. Was she actually tongue-tied over seeing him?

A relaxed smile now replaced his surprised look. He nodded toward the door and continued whispering. "Do you have a minute to chat?"

She returned his nod and followed him into the hall.

In the brightly lit hallway, he went straight to the point. "I'm sorry we didn't get to meet back at the bar. Any chance you'd like to grab a cup of coffee sometime?"

Her heart pounded. Why did this guy affect her like this? She felt like a schoolgirl who had been kissed for the first time. Get a grip. Words tumbled out. "Today is pretty full, but tonight I'm meeting my friend Teri and her boyfriend for a drink. Would you like to join us?"

His face lit up with a smile that made her go weak in the knees. What in the world had she just done? The guy suggested a casual coffee meeting and she'd turned it into a double date with her best friend. Before she could retract her offer, he replied, "Sure. That would be great. Same place?"

"Yes. Seven o'clock."

"Great, I'll see you tonight. By the way, I'm RT. It might be nice to know your name too." He extended his hand.

She laughed and shook his hand. "Nice to meet you. I'm Ashley."

"I look forward to seeing you tonight, Ashley." As he moved to depart, his eyes lingered. Her heart felt like it was in her throat. She swallowed and gave him a slight wave.

Lost in thought, she almost forgot to report back for her hearing. That is exactly why she didn't need a relationship. It would only complicate her life. She had other priorities. Tonight, she'd make it clear. A glass of wine with a new friend. Nothing more, but if that was true, why did she feel so giddy?

12

SARAH

After leaving the cemetery, Sarah knew what needed to be done. She needed to get in contact with her children and find an attorney. That started with making a call to the caseworker. Where could she find a phone booth? If she remembered right, there was one at the gas station in the next block. As she got closer, she glanced at the back of the lot. Sure enough. She parked her car and walked to the booth.

Stepping inside, she pushed the hinged door to close it. She reached into her purse and pulled out the card that Julie from Child Protective Services gave her. Dropping a few coins into the slot, she dialed the number, and waited as the phone rang. When a woman answered, Sarah introduced herself and went right to the point. "When can I see my children?"

"One step at a time Mrs. Thornton. There is a parenting plan you'll need to review and sign. I've also put together a schedule to see your children. For now, we'll start with Mondays, Wednesdays, and Fridays from 3:00 - 4:00. Will that work for you?"

Sarah sucked in a sharp breath. Only three hours a week to see her children? "Can I see them now?"

"No, they are in foster homes. Out of courtesy to the foster families, we need to make arrangements in advance so they can bring them to our office. You can meet them here where you will be able to see them under the supervision of our staff."

Sarah's mind reeled. Supervision? Why did she have to be supervised? Why couldn't they just come home? What made them think she might harm them? And to mention courtesy to the foster family? What about courtesy to her, their mother? She dared not speak any of that. She needed to keep her cool.

Again, she took a breath. "I'll do whatever is necessary to see them whenever possible."

"Great. With that resolved, let's set a time when we can go over the parenting plan." The woman sounded more enthusiastic than appropriate under the circumstances.

Sarah agreed upon a time and hung up the phone. She shook her head. How was she going to manage this? With a week off for Noah's funeral. she couldn't afford any more time away, especially with Tyler in jail. She needed to work as much as possible to support them. If she couldn't keep up with the mortgage and car payments, they would be without a home or transportation. Where would they be then?

She looked out the phone booth window and watched the traffic. All those people going about their lives, doing their daily tasks. She sighed and let her breath come out slowly. She felt a tear run down her cheek, but swiped it away. There was no time for tears. Arrangements needed to be made for the upcoming appointments. Dropping more coins into the slot, she dialed her boss's number. He answered on the second ring.

"Mr. Thomas, it's Sarah."

"Oh Sarah. I am so sorry about your son's death."

"Thank you." Her voice shook. She took a breath. How much should she tell him?

Mr. Thomas filled the empty space. "Is there anything we can do here at the nursing home?"

Her throat felt tight. She should have stopped in to see him rather than trying to talk over the phone.

He must have been uncomfortable with the silence. He jumped back into the conversation. "The patients miss you. They are asking about you. When do you think you'll return?" She heard him gasp. "Oh, I'm sorry. Perhaps you aren't ready. I don't want to rush you."

She leaned to rest her forehead on the glass. It felt warm and seemed to calm her. "No, I need to get back to work. I'm in a difficult position though. I need to change my schedule."

"Change your schedule?"

"Yes. Our tragedy..." She took a deep breath and looked out toward the parking lot. She noticed a man sitting in his car. He must be waiting to use the phone. She turned her back to the door. She needed to come up with an explanation. "Ryan and Leanna, I must spend time with them. They get out of school at 3:00. If I could work a split shift so I have a couple hours off then, it would really help."

"Of course. Of course. We can work that out." His voice sounded edgy; not like he was mad, more like he just wanted to end the conversation. She felt sorry for him. What more can one say to an employee who just buried their son?

"Thank you. I really appreciate it. I will be back to work next week. Again, thank you for understanding."

As she placed the hand piece in the receiver, it felt like it weighed ten pounds. She sighed, leaned back against the door, and closed her eyes. The past week had taken a toll. The phone booth provided a warm cocoon. Running her fingers through her hair, she tried to consider her next move. Perhaps she could find an attorney in the yellow pages. She reached for the phone book that hung by a chain. Before she could flip to "Attorneys" in the directory, a sharp tap on the glass made her jump. She found herself facing the man from the car.

"You done here? I need to make a call."

She nodded and unhinged the door to leave. She could look for an attorney when she got home. She certainly didn't have the energy to stand her ground in a phone booth with this guy.

* * * * *

When Sarah pulled into her driveway, she noticed the mailman on her step. He waved at her. "Hi there. I have a certified letter for you. Glad you're here."

She tried to smile as she thanked him. He had no idea the horror playing out in her life. Taking the envelope, she noticed the Coroner's Office stamped in the upper left corner. Her hand trembled as she signed on the line and thanked the mailman.

Unlocking the door, she let herself into the house. She sat down at the kitchen table and fingered the envelope. Was she ready to read the report? Could she handle this? Alone? Then again, no point in delaying it. She slid her finger under the flap, opened the envelope, and removed the letter. She took her time unfolding the crisp folds. The report confirmed what Julie at CPS stated. Cause of death: Secondary drowning. She had never heard of that. What did that mean? Where could she find out? She thought about the encyclopedias her parents passed onto her. Although they were a bit dated, it's the best resource she could think of.

Standing to retrieve the encyclopedia, she looked out the window. Her neighbors, April and George were just pulling into their driveway. George was a doctor. Surely, he would know. She grabbed her sweater and headed out the door, waving at them before they got to their front door. "I'm sorry to bother you."

April's eyes were downcast as she reached out to Sarah to give her a hug. "No bother Sarah. Is there anything we can do to help?"

"I am reading the coroner's report." She felt a catch in her throat. She couldn't say Noah's name. It hurt too much. She paused to gather herself. "George, could you tell me what it means?"

"Of course. Come in and I'll look at it with you."

They led her to their oak kitchen table. As George retrieved his reading glasses, April poured glasses of ice tea. April reached for Sarah's hand, holding it while her lip trembled. Sarah looked away. She knew she would cry if she looked into April's sad eyes.

George sat down in a chair and reached across the table, taking the envelope. He read in silence. When he got to the end, he cleared his throat. "It appears Noah died from Secondary Drowning."

She shook her head, waiting for him to finish.

"It's very rare, Sarah. I personally don't think I've ever seen a case. Essentially, after a water submersion, a small amount of water can get into the lungs and cause inflammation. That in turn, can cause difficulty breathing. The symptoms can be subtle. Coughing, wheezing, vomiting, shallow breathing, sleepiness."

She inhaled sharply as she heard the words coughing and sleepiness. Noah coughed and had been sleepy when they returned from the pool, but that was to be expected after a morning in the sun. She hadn't felt any sense of alarm nor suspected he was ill. Thinking of Noah and their last moments together, her eyes filled with tears. She looked down at the table. "I had no idea." Her words came out in a whisper. She cleared her throat and raised her eyes to look at George. "The children told me Noah went under the water, but it sounded like it was no big deal." A rattled breath escaped her. "What kind of a mother am I that I didn't notice my son was... DYING?"

"Oh, Sarah," April rose to put her arms around her. "It sounds like it is very hard to know."

"Yes Sarah," George added, "Like I said, it is very rare. You couldn't have known. You can't blame yourself."

"They have arrested Tyler."

George and April both gasped. "Why?"

"They said Tyler neglected him. In fact, they are saying I did too. They took Ryan and Leanna. They are in foster homes."

"What? I've never heard of such a thing." George's voice escalated to a near shout. His face turned red. A vein in his neck started to twitch. "I can't imagine they would hold Tyler responsible, or anyone for that matter."

"I agree. I've been told to get a lawyer." She struggled to hold her emotions in check.

April's eyes were wide in horror. Her words came out in gasps. "Oh, Sarah. Your sweet children must be so scared. I'm so sorry Sarah. I don't even know what to say."

Sarah didn't respond. She stared at the clock on the dining room wall. Time seemed to stand still. How did this happen? They were just a normal family raising their children in a normal neighborhood. At any moment, she expected to wake up and find their normal life back to normal. She shook her head and rose to leave. Nothing more could be accomplished here. "Thank you both. I need to be going."

"Oh Sarah, we will be praying for this to be resolved quickly." April squeezed her hand.

Sarah paused at the front door. They gave her a hug. "Please let us know if we can do anything."

"Thank you. I will." She took one step off the porch, stopped and turned back to George. "I don't know why I didn't think to ask. Do you happen to know a good attorney?"

"Yes, as a matter of fact, I do. I'll make some calls to see if someone I know can help you."

"Thank you. I really don't know if we can afford one."

"I'll ask around."

"Again, thank you."

As she stepped off the porch, she looked across the street toward her own home. She will be alone again tonight. The thought seemed to sit in her stomach like bad food. To think just days ago, she'd excused herself from a family outing to have time alone to get her housework done. What she wouldn't do to take that day back. To keep her family safe at home. To give up her time alone forever, but that day was gone. Today it felt like "alone" would be her life sentence.

She scolded herself. She couldn't think like that. She had to get Ryan and Leanna back home. She had to get Tyler back home. Then she thought of Noah. Rushing up the final steps into her house, she burst through the door, stumbled to the living room, slumped onto the couch, and let herself fall apart. Noah, sweet Noah. She would never get him back home again.

13

ASHLEY

After her brief encounter with RT in the courthouse, Ashley called Teri to let her know there would be an additional guest. Teri gushed with excitement, but Ashley quickly put things in perspective. "Don't be getting me married off yet."

"Who said anything about marriage? I'm just thrilled you are considering a life outside of work."

"I'm just saying…"

"Don't worry. I will behave. I won't start talking about being your maid of honor yet."

Ashley smiled as she hung up the phone. How she loved Teri. Being with Teri and Eric would make for easier conversation. This would be fun. She felt happy, happier than she'd felt in months.

The afternoon couldn't go fast enough. At 4:30 she closed her last file and left the office. She'd put in many late nights in the past few weeks so leaving early tonight was acceptable. Besides, she wanted to freshen up, maybe put on that new dress she'd never gotten around to wearing. Again, she reminded herself. Wine with a new friend. Nothing more.

At home, she took longer than she intended getting ready, examining herself in the mirror way too many times. She put her long brown hair up in a bun, then pulled it out, and put it in a ponytail. By the time she walked out of the apartment, her hair hung straight down her back. She chided herself for being pokey. She hoped she would get there before RT so he wouldn't be alone with Eric and Teri. That might be uncomfortable.

When she arrived, Teri greeted her with a hug and a giddy wiggle of excitement. Ashley gave her a wink and turned to say hello to Eric. They barely finished their greetings when RT walked through the door and strode to their table. His eyes met Ashley's. "It's nice to see you. Thank you for the invitation." He turned and reached out his hand toward Eric, introduced himself, and then greeted Teri. "Perhaps I could buy the first round of drinks?"

"Thank you. That would be very nice."

As they settled around the table, Ashley could feel him watching her. A familiar warmth came into her cheeks. Maybe it was just the heat in the room. It felt hotter than usual. The temperature was always a bit unpredictable as summer moved to fall.

Soon conversation was underway. The men found common ground as they talked of cars and football. She learned RT graduated from law school and joined a firm in the last few years. Teri made frequent comments under her breath to Ashley, indicating she approved.

An hour passed with ease. RT shifted in his seat and looked at her. When their eyes met, it felt like just the two of them there. He eased into more personal questions. "Are you from around here?"

"Yes, I've been here all my life. My parents...umm. My mom still lives here." Sadness welled inside when she corrected herself, speaking only of her mom.

RT didn't seem to notice. "So, why were you at the courthouse today?"

"I was there to testify on a case. I'm a caseworker for CPS."

"Oh! Really?" His inquisitive smile dissolved. His eyes grew serious. He pulled back from the table as if to put distance between them. Unsure why his demeanor changed, she attempted to pull Eric and Teri back into the conversation. They were hardcore Seahawks fans, rarely missing a game. Trying to revive the fun of the night, she talked of the upcoming game, but something changed. He seemed distant.

Ashley felt uncomfortable as a weight of sadness came over her. She fought the urge to flee. She had to get out of this situation before the tears she felt welling in her eyes came to the surface. She pushed her chair back and stood. "You know, I'm beat. I need to call it a night."

Teri stared at her. Her eyes went wide with the question she dared not ask out loud: "What are you doing?"

She returned Teri's look with an apologetic squint.

RT seemed ready to have the evening over as well. He also stood and pulled his suit jacket from the back of the chair. "Yes, I need to get an early start tomorrow too. Thanks for inviting me." His words lacked enthusiasm. "I'll walk out with you."

Ashley said her goodbyes and followed him to the door where he stood waiting. Once outside, he walked her to her car in an awkward silence.

She walked faster than intended, wanting to get this over. When they reached her car, she spoke. "I enjoyed getting to know you."

"Yes, it was a pleasure." He paused, then added, "Maybe I'll see you again in court?"

"I hope so." Another awkward pause. "Thank you for joining us. I hope you have a good night."

"Yes, thank you. Goodnight." He gave her a slight wave, turned and walked away.

She slid into her car, turned on the ignition, and watched in her rearview mirror as he got in his car and pulled out of the parking lot. She took a deep breath as she tried to sort out her feelings. Disappointment? Sadness? Uncertainty? The evening hadn't gone as she'd hoped and yet, wasn't this exactly what she'd wanted? A glass of wine with a new friend. Nothing more. So why were tears streaming down her face right now?

14

RT

As RT drove away from the parking lot, he felt like a lost boy. He slammed his fist into the steering wheel as an old sense of defeat crept into his heart.

He drove home in silence, choosing to keep the radio off. He took the interstate so he could avoid most of the traffic lights. Besides, he wouldn't have to focus so much on driving since he traveled this route often.

The streetlights seemed to call out the darkness that lurked in him. He felt embarrassed by the way he'd reacted. Even more though, he felt a sense of disbelief. He thought he'd dealt with it. He thought he'd healed and put it behind him. If nothing else, he thought he'd outrun it all. Obviously, he had more work to do before he could accept what happened.

As if a chisel bore a hole into his steel shell of protection, old feelings of regret and shame filled his mind, but those days were over. He had put it behind him. He had moved on and made something of himself. He'd become an attorney, for goodness sakes. If that didn't prove it, what would? So why this mental battle once again?

He shook his head to clear his mind and took a deep breath. He needed to rein in his thoughts. No point going there again.

He thought of Ashley. He really liked her. Classy yet humble. And pretty. Very pretty, but there was more. What was it about her? Authentic. Yes. That best described her. Not flaky like so many women he knew, especially once they found out what he did for a living. They seemed overly impressed he was an attorney. They made suggestive advances which made him uncomfortable. Ashley seemed different. He felt at ease with her. He wanted to get to know her better, but what were the chances now? He had blown it tonight.

He thought of when he saw her in the courtroom. He'd assumed she was a fellow attorney. They would have that in common. Instead, she worked as a caseworker for CPS! He couldn't believe it. When would he ever learn that one should never make assumptions?

Yet, even with that information, deep regret snuck into his gut. He hadn't even gotten her phone number. He needed to call her, if for no other reason than to apologize. It had been a good evening right up until that moment, and he enjoyed meeting Teri and Eric. They hit it off. He reprimanded himself again for behaving so poorly. He felt a sting in his eyes. When would it ever stop hurting? When would he just get over it? He shook his head to clear his mind.

He sighed as he once again attempted to box away the thoughts that erupted, but the one thought he didn't want to get out of his mind was Ashley. No matter what, he needed to see her again. Perhaps they would meet again in the courtroom. Maybe he could stop at the bar again on another night and find her there. If he had to, he could call the CPS office, but he'd have to be pretty desperate to do that.

15

SARAH

Tyler's hearing was scheduled for the next afternoon. Sarah stopped at the jail that morning to share what she'd learned about the three attorneys their neighbor George recommended. When escorted to his holding cell, she couldn't seem to meet his eyes. She already knew how he'd react, but she had to tell him.

"Tyler, I made some calls for an attorney." She paused to gather her courage, then just blurted it out. "Standard hourly fees are $150 an hour. They said a full trial could run anywhere from $24,000 to $50,000. Plus, there's a $2,000 retainer fee." Tears welled in her eyes as she shared the news.

Tyler's eyes widened in disbelief. "What? We can't afford that."

"We've got some money saved." She bit her lip as she looked at the floor.

"Not that much."

Her eyes met his. She felt like she was begging for her own life. "Maybe we could take out a loan. I could pick up extra shifts. Get a second job."

"NO!" The intensity and volume of his voice caused her to jerk. "That's beyond our ability to ever pay back. You can't pick up a minimum wage job at four dollars an hour to cover those costs."

She remained silent, fighting back tears as she waited for him to come up with a better idea.

He clenched his hands on the bars of the cell. His words seemed weighed with uncertainty. "When they read me my rights, they told me if I couldn't afford an attorney, they would appoint one for me."

She nodded. "Will you be well-represented?"

He shook his head and let out a long low sigh. He lifted his eyes to meet hers. They looked vacant. "We don't have a choice." His monotone response reflected his level of despair.

It didn't feel right, but she knew there would be no changing Tyler's mind. He was right. They didn't have that kind of money.

Their time together was brief. The policeman escorted her out. She had a couple hours to kill before the hearing, but going home felt too sad. She drove to the courthouse and sat in her car, allowing her mind to wander. Then she went into the courtroom and found an empty bench at the back of the room.

When the bailiff called Tyler's case, Tyler shuffled in from a back room. Seeing him, she sat upright and strained to make eye contact. When his eyes met hers, she bit her bottom lip to keep from crying. She must be strong.

The prosecutor presented his statement, charging Tyler with negligent homicide and child neglect.

The judge gazed at Tyler and sighed, "Do you have an attorney?"

"No, we can't afford one."

"Very well. One will be appointed." He nodded toward a man sitting in the courtroom. "I am assigning you to Don Webber. You can meet with him before deciding your plea."

The guard led Tyler from the room. His new attorney followed. Sarah didn't know what to do. Should she follow them? Could she be there during the conversation? She'd never been through something like this. Before she could decide, the judge called another case so she remained seated, feeling as if her body were in cement.

Fifteen minutes passed. The guard led Tyler back into the room. The judge noted his arrival and nodded, indicating he should step forward.

"Mr. Thornton, you've met with your attorney. What do you plead?"

"Not guilty, your honor." His voice cracked.

The judge turned to the prosecutor and addressed him. "What sort of bail do you recommend?"

"Your honor, this is a very serious crime. I recommend Mr. Thornton be remanded without bail until his trial."

Sarah gasped. Why would they hold him in jail? He didn't have a criminal record and Noah's death was an accident. Still trying to process what happened, she didn't hear Mr. Webber's response although it didn't seem to have any influence. The judge lowered his gavel and ordered Tyler to jail until his trial.

Tyler stood and looked over his shoulder at her. His lips and chin were trembling. She extended her hands toward him even though they would never reach across the room. Then he was gone.

16

ASHLEY

Ashley glanced up as the secretary placed another new case file on her desk. That made two new cases this week alone. The yellow sticky note she'd attached to the corner of her computer caught her eye. It read: FOR THE CHILDREN. She'd put it there as a reminder to always work for the best interests of the children she served. It had become a habit to read it every time she started a new case. She moved to open one of the files. As she did, her phone rang. She sighed with weary resignation and answered it. She recognized Melissa's voice and her spirits lifted.

Melissa and Nathan foster-parented a five-year-old little guy named Michael for a year. When he became available to adopt, they welcomed him into their family. Even though the adoption was finalized several years ago, Melissa kept in touch. Ashley always loved to hear from them. They were one of the families who reminded her that her hard work mattered, in a way, her reward. Knowing a child like Michael had a family to call his own.

As soon as they greeted one another, Melissa grew quiet.

"Is there something wrong Melissa?" Her stomach tightened as if sensing bad news.

"Nathan...Nathan and I are getting a divorce." Sobs followed.

"What? Oh no. I'm so sorry."

Melissa paused to take a breath then plowed on. She seemed determined to finish. "Our marriage has been in trouble for quite a while. We both hoped having a child would make it better, but it didn't. Michael's issues have added to the problem."

"There are services to help you. I would be happy to refer you."

"No, it's too late. Nathan is finished. He left."

"I'm so sorry." Ashley hesitated. She cleared her throat and asked the only thing that came to mind. "What are your plans for parenting Michael?"

"Michael never seemed to bond with us. Neither of us want to take him on by ourselves."

"What are you saying?" A chill ran down Ashley's back.

"I know it sounds horrible, but he's so much harder than we thought." Melissa paused. "Maybe we weren't supposed to adopt him. I just think he'd be better off with another family."

Ashley realized she'd been holding her breath. She exhaled knowing this conversation was far from over. The next question seemed to stick in her throat. Words came out in halted chunks. "Melissa, are you saying... Do you want... Are you wanting to relinquish your parental rights?"

"Yes." Melissa's voice dropped to a whisper.

Stunned silence followed. Ashley felt like she'd been kicked in the stomach. A wave of nausea hit her. How could they give away their son? How could they give him back to the state, knowing he would go back into foster care? Worse, how could SHE have failed so miserably in placing Michael? A feeling of doom came over her and another thought filled her with horror: How many other children had she failed by placing them with the wrong families?

Ashley had to maintain a professional presence. "Melissa, when do you want to relinquish Michael?"

"As soon as possible."

The muscles in Ashley's jaw tightened. She shoved the feelings of dismay aside. This was her job. "Okay. I'll arrange for a foster family. There will be documents to sign."

"I understand."

Ashley paused. She didn't know if she should say it, but it only seemed right to defend Michael. "I hope you understand he may never find another adoptive family. Not after going through a failed adoption. He's seven now too, which makes him harder to place."

"I'm sorry. I'm so sorry." The phone went dead.

The dial tone echoed in Ashley's ear. She hesitated to hang up her end. Pulling the phone away from her ear, she stared at it. What just happened? How did this happen? Oh, poor Michael. She set the phone down and sat at her desk in stunned disbelief. The magnitude of her role seemed unbearable. It was as if she played God, matching children with families. She wasn't qualified. This was more authority than anyone should have. And little Michael. Her heart ached. He might never trust another adult. Ever.

17

ASHLEY

Ashley felt numb as she went about the rest of her morning. Early in the afternoon, her supervisor Robin came into her office with an urgent report of child abuse. "I'd like you to address this today." Ashley still hadn't gotten used to the direct manner of her new supervisor.

Ashley sighed and Robin paused. "Is there a problem?"

Ashley straightened in her chair and lifted her eyes. "No. I'll get right to this."

Robin remained standing at the door. "Are you having trouble keeping up with your cases?"

"Yes... No..." She paused. "I'm sorry. It's not that." Ashley didn't feel like sharing yet, but knew she had to say something. "I took a difficult call this morning." The sting of Melissa's call made her feel like she would cry.

Robin stepped toward Ashley's desk. Her eyes dropped to the desktop and roamed across it. She looked at Ashley. "You're an experienced caseworker. Difficult how?"

"An adoption fell through." The moment the words were out, she wished she could take them back.

"With a child you placed?"

"Yes, several years ago." Her face felt hot. Her hands were clammy. She picked up a pen and rolled it between her fingers.

The lines in Robin's face deepened and she leaned over Ashley's desk. "I expect a report on my desk by tomorrow."

"Of course. I'll check out this case first and then get to work on the reports."

Robin turned on her heel and left. Ashley let out a sigh of relief. The intensity around the office had grown in the months since Robin became the supervisor. That wasn't all. She didn't like feeling under a microscope. This job was hard enough. A feeling of doom settled in her gut. She tried to shake it. Regardless of the conflict she felt, she owed it to the next child to be there for them.

Ashley grabbed her jacket and headed to her car. Although she should have asked another caseworker to go with her, she needed time alone. The drive would help to clear her head. She checked the address and maneuvered her car out of the parking lot onto the street. Twenty minutes later, she pulled up to the curb. She wasn't sure how she got there. It seemed her mind failed to follow her out of the office. She needed to pull herself together.

She glanced at the trailer house to confirm the address and noticed a little boy sitting alone on the front steps, shivering. He wasn't wearing a coat even though a chill hung in the air. He couldn't have been more than four.

She got out of her car and started toward the house. She could hear someone shouting from inside. She made eye contact with the little boy. "Hi there." His eyes widened. He rose to his feet and without saying a word, opened the door and vanished inside. She could hear more sharp words. It sounded like they were directed at the little boy. She walked to the door and gave it a firm knock.

A man shoved the door open. "What do you want?" His shout caused spit to spray onto her face. It scared her, but she refused to show it. She should have asked a coworker to come with her, but it was too late for that now. Not likely any of the other caseworkers were free anyway with all the extra cases this week.

On reflex, she wiped the spit off her face and then extended her hand and introduced herself. "My name is Ashley. I'm with Child

Protective Services. There has been a report. I need to check on your son."

"Report, huh?" The man's words caused him to spat again. He glared at her extended hand, but didn't reach out to shake it.

"Is there anyone else here with you?"

"Yes! Why?" He looked down at her while rubbing his unshaven chin.

"I'd like to speak to anyone in the house."

He stepped aside and let her enter. She hovered near the door. If she needed to leave, she didn't want to be far from the exit. She glanced around, taking it all in. A television blared. Empty beer cans were strewn on the floor. Cigarette butts filled a dish on the coffee table. Near the back of the living room, a woman stood with her back to the wall. Streaks of mascara left a black trail down her face. She wiped the back of her hand over her face.

The man bellowed, "John, get in here." Soon the little boy stood in the room, his chin hanging on his chest.

Ashley clutched the key ring in her jacket pocket. She could feel her breaths quicken. The man seemed to jerk as he paced the floor. He might be high on something. She needed to get out of this situation. She didn't feel safe.

The woman spoke. "Are you here to take John to a foster home? Cause if you are, that's fine. He'd be better off." With that she grabbed a plastic bag and gathered together clothes from the backs of chairs and out of a pile on the floor. She shoved it at the boy. "Now you go. Be a good boy. Do what this nice lady says."

Ashley sensed that, in a strange way, the woman might be trying to protect John. She took John's hand and led him to the door. Now that he stood closer, she could see bruises on his face. John didn't say a word as she led him out of the house. Tears made tracks down his face.

At the car, she stooped to look him in the eyes. "You're going to be okay." John didn't look at her. She opened the car, helped him get settled into the backseat, and buckled him in. When she straightened up, she saw the woman standing in the door, holding it open. Ashley made eye contact and walked closer. She tried to keep her voice quiet so the man wouldn't hear. "Do you need help? Are you being abused?"

The woman flicked her hand at Ashley. "Hell no. Now get out of here. And don't bring that brat back."

Without another word, Ashley turned and walked to her car. As she got in, she let out a pent-up breath. She was more terrified than she wanted to admit. She gripped the steering wheel to stop her hands from shaking and then turned to look at John in the backseat. "I am going to help you." Again, he didn't respond.

Although she had developed thick skin over the years, this was something she could never understand. How could a parent be so unattached to their own child? How could they turn their backs on their own flesh and blood? Every child deserves to be loved. She would do everything in her power to make sure they were. It was the one way she could repay her debt to someone who had done the same for her.

As she drove back across town with the silent little boy in her backseat, she thought of the many children she'd removed from their homes. Some were like this little guy, unable to even express his feelings. Others ran to the car and jostled with each other as if they were going on a big adventure. Still others screamed and fought her, angry about being taken. She couldn't blame them. They didn't understand. The chaos and volatility of abuse or neglect was all they'd ever known.

Reflecting on these scenarios, she found herself wondering again: Were her biological parents like the ones she just met? Did they just give her away and ask that she not be returned? Somehow, she needed to find out why she'd been given up for adoption, yet she feared knowing too. Maybe she shouldn't pursue answers to her questions, but this ache in her heart since her dad died just wouldn't go away.

18

ASHLEY

Back at the office, Ashley directed John to a child size chair and table and offered him crayons and paper. He didn't seem to notice. He stared off into the distance. Then she called the police to file a police report about John. The police were supposed to be present when she did a removal, but under the circumstances, she wasn't going to stick around. With the police report done, she set about finding John a foster home. She hated making calls with him in hearing distance, but she had no choice. Until she could find a foster home, he needed to be right here with her.

Her first four calls were unsuccessful. Finally, she got a yes with her fifth call. She hung up the phone and knelt to John's level. "John, I have found a family that will keep you safe. They are looking forward to meeting you." He never lifted his face to meet her eyes. She took his hand and led him to her car. He remained silent as they drove to the home, even as she introduced him to his foster mom. He seemed empty of all emotion.

As she drove away from the foster home, her thoughts remained on John. She wondered when he'd start speaking. Sometimes it took months. So much trauma. So much damage. Even being removed from an abusive home created trauma. From a child's perspective, their own dysfunctional home seemed better than being with a stranger in a strange home.

At the office, she hung her jacket on the hook and sank into her chair. The familiar sticky note seemed to mock her. FOR THE CHILDREN. Yes, it was always about the children, but why was

Denise E. Johnson

her job even necessary? Why did people even have children if they didn't want them? Why did people who wanted them struggle with infertility? Life wasn't fair, especially for children. Families didn't function like they should, or at least how she thought they should, but personal biases or opinions had no place in her role as a professional caseworker.

She took a deep breath and turned her attention back to her desk. Mulling over the brokenness of life wouldn't accomplish anything. With John now safe, she needed to find a home for Michael. She started back through her list of foster homes. Just as she reached for the phone, it rang. Another typical nonstop day. Melissa's call crossed her mind. She hesitated before answering. She couldn't take another hard conversation today.

Another foster mom, Heather, greeted her. Her voice bubbled with joy. "I just had to share the good news. Thad's twelve-month appointment went great today. He has caught up to average weight and height!"

Ashley's body relaxed; the pent-up pressure released. "What good news. I'm so glad you called." She could use some good news.

Heather gushed. "The doctor was so pleased, especially considering how small he was at birth. He didn't see any ongoing side effects from the meth use during Thad's mother's pregnancy and the fetal alcohol issues are minimal."

"That's fabulous Heather. You're doing a great job." If only there were more foster moms like Heather.

"Oh, and he took his first steps yesterday." Ashley could hear Heather take a deep sigh. "Dave and I love him so much." Her words were heavy with emotion.

"I know you do." Her heart ached for them. As Thad's only parents since his birth, they hoped to adopt him.

"Um. How's his mom doing? Has she been able to stay sober?" Heather's voice sounded timid, as if unsure she wanted to hear the answer.

Ashley tried to be upfront about each circumstance while maintaining client confidentiality. She knew Heather and Dave loved Thad as much as any parent could. "She's still in treatment, but it's not going well. I can't promise anything Heather."

"I know."

"Thad needs a stable home and I'm not sure his mom is going to be able to provide that. I don't want you to get your hopes up yet. We need to give this more time."

"I understand."

Ashley needed to get off the phone. She didn't want to mislead Heather by saying more than she should. "Thanks for the wonderful update on Thad, Heather. I'll come by next week and maybe I'll know more then."

As she hung up the phone, she let out a deep breath. This job was tough. The best interests of the children weren't always black and white. While parents went through treatment to become sober and healthy, their children were growing up in foster care and developing new attachments. It was the children who paid for their parent's mistakes.

She glanced at the clock on her wall. Six p.m. She should call it a day. It had been a hard, emotional one. She locked her computer and headed down the hall, passing Robin's office. The light was still on. Ashley poked her head in.

"Goodnight Robin." She tried to sound upbeat.

"Did you get that report done for me?" Robin's voice clipped with impatience.

"I'll have it ready in the morning."

"Good, I'll expect it then."

Ashley nodded and turned back toward the hall. She needed to get home and decompress. Fortunately, home was only twenty minutes away. She appreciated her four-plex and the safe neighborhood. Swiping her card, the security gate rose and she drove through. She parked her car under the carport and made her way up the steps to her apartment. After letting herself in, she tossed her keys on the counter and considered what she would make for dinner. Leftover stew would have to do. She popped it in the microwave and decided to lie down for a few minutes while it heated. Kicking off her shoes, she reclined on the sofa. That was the last thing she remembered before sleep claimed her exhausted body.

19

SARAH

Sarah's new reality became a familiar routine. A month passed since the day of Tyler's arrest; the day the children were taken away. At work, she couldn't seem to focus as she went about the tasks of bathing her patients during morning rounds. Today she would get to see the children. When her first shift ended, she hurried to her car. She wanted to be there before they arrived.

At the CPS office, she could hear typewriter keys clicking in the background. She shuttered a bit. She hated typing classes in high school. That's one of the reasons she decided to become a CNA. She worked better with people than machines.

The caseworker directed her to the room where she and the children always met. She looked at the plaid, thread-worn couch before sitting. She hated to even touch it. It had to be filthy from so many parents and children meeting here through the weeks. She sat anyway. She turned her attention to the one-way mirror. Someone would be watching their every move. Such a violation of her private time with her children. Tapping her toe, she waited for them.

Moments later, Ryan and Leanna burst through the door. "Mama, Mama." Both clung to her. Ryan rubbed his eyes with his fists and tried to hide his tears. Leanna didn't bother as hers flowed. Sarah gathered them into her arms and breathed deeply. How good to be together. She knelt to get eye level with them. "My loves. Look at you. I can hardly believe my eyes. Ryan, you must have grown an inch since I last saw you." She smoothed his hair and then rested the palm of her hand on his cheek. "And Leanna, my little button." She lifted Leanna up. "Could you get any cuter? Oh, how I've missed you both."

Leanna clutched her neck. Sarah glanced down at Ryan. His eyes were sad. She leaned to give him an extra hug. "Are you doing okay?" He nodded and turned to sit on the couch. She attempted to put Leanna on the floor, but she held tight. She needed to find out what was going on with Ryan. "Look what I brought from home Ryan. Your favorite board game." Leanna was too small for it yet, so she brought one of her dolls and some toys. Seeing the dolls, Leanna loosened her grip and began playing, but Ryan remained on the couch. "Ryan, would you like to play?"

"I never liked that game." He scowled and frowned at her.

"What do you mean son? We play it all the time."

He pulled his knees to his chest and turned his back to her. "I don't want to play it."

She sat next to him and pulled him close. He resisted at first, but then relaxed, allowing his body to nestle against hers. Soon soft sobs escaped him. Leanna looked up and came to sit next to them. She patted his leg. Her eyes looked like they would spill tears again. For a time, the three of them sat in silence as Sarah wrestled with what to say to help her children. Before long, Leanna became bored and went to play with her doll again.

"Mommy, I want to come home." Ryan's comment caught her heart. She gulped to keep from crying.

"I know. Soon son. I'm working hard to get you and Leanna home."

"Why can't we come home now? Why did we have to leave?" He asked every time they met in the past weeks, but each time it became harder to answer. None of it made sense to her either.

"There was a misunderstanding. We are doing everything we can, so we can bring you home as soon as possible."

A few moments later, Ryan slid off the couch and sat on the floor in front of the game. "I guess we might as well play."

She smiled. "What a great idea." They played the game in a small huddle of love with Leanna next to them. The hour passed in what felt like minutes.

When the door swung open, a caseworker stood there. "Children, time to go. Say goodbye to your mother."

Ryan jumped to his feet and wrapped his arms around her waist. "Mom, please don't leave." Leanna dropped her toys in mid-play and began to cry, murmuring, "Mommy. Mommy."

"I will be back. I'll always come back. And soon, we'll all go home together."

"You promise?" Ryan's gaze could have drilled a hole through concrete.

"Yes, I promise." With that she placed kisses on her children's faces. "I'll see you in a few days. Be good. I love you."

"Come with me now children." The caseworker briskly escorted them from the room.

Sarah stood in the doorway and waved goodbye. She didn't want her children to think she left them, so she stood there, waiting until they were out of sight. If they turned around, she wanted to be the last thing they saw. It took every ounce of restraint to not run down the hall, grab them, and escape.

When the children left the building, another caseworker, Anne, stepped into the hallway. "Mrs. Thornton. I need to have a word with you."

"Sure." Something about Anne's tone made Sarah nervous.

Anne stepped closer. "You cannot continue to make false promises to your children."

"What do you mean?" Sarah frowned.

"Telling your children you'll be taking them home soon."

Sarah tilted her head and pursed her lips. She cleared her throat and answered cautiously. "Isn't that the truth? Isn't that what we're working towards?"

Anne crossed her arms. "It's yet to be determined, but you're making it harder on your children by promising something that isn't certain yet."

Sarah bit her lip. She could feel her cheeks burning. "What more can I do to get them home?"

"It's up to the court." Her words stung like a slap on the face. The thought of the courts turned Sarah's stomach. Tyler's hearing landed him in jail with no trial date set yet. Sarah didn't have much faith in the courts.

She looked at Anne who leaned against the door frame, arms crossed, as if challenging Sarah to do the wrong thing. Sarah let out a sigh. Nothing more could be accomplished with this conversation. Besides, it was time to get back to work. "Thank you for your concern." It came out with more sarcasm than Sarah intended.

20

RT

Several weeks had passed since RT met Ashley and her friends for a glass of wine. She hadn't left his mind. He hoped to have connected with her by now. Maybe he would have to make that dreaded call to CPS.

When he reached the top of the stairs, he looked across the crowded hallway. There she was, at the far end of the hall. He headed straight for her. She seemed to have noticed him so he smiled and waved. She looked away. A sick feeling filled his stomach. That wasn't the reaction he'd hoped for. Sidestepping through the crowd, he determined to make his way to her.

When he got close, he smiled again. He hoped he'd get a different response. "Hey, it's good to see you."

She returned a stiff, formal smile.

He ignored it. "I've wanted to get in touch with you. I owe you an apology."

"No need." Ashley brushed her hand in the air.

He held up his hands. "No please, I'd like to explain. I had a great time. It's just, well, I've got some, uh, baggage. I thought I'd dealt with it. I guess I haven't."

Her expression softened. He continued, not wanting to lose her attention. "Anyway, we don't have to talk about that." He laughed. "Could I take you out to dinner to make up for my bad behavior?"

She met his eyes and gave a hesitant nod.

"Great. Where is your favorite restaurant?"

Her eyes became thin slits and response came out in a slow drawl. "Where's your favorite restaurant? That's where I'd like to go."

Not the answer he'd expected. "Okay. That's fair. I love Louie's Pasta Bar. Ever been there?"

She shook her head. "No, I can't say I have but I love pasta."

Great. He was making progress. "So how about tomorrow at 7?"

"That will work."

So pleased with himself, he started to give her a hug, but then stopped. That would be inappropriate so early in a relationship, but he couldn't keep the smile from his face. "It's settled. I'll meet you there tomorrow night."

"Sounds good." The cautious smile she gave him made him realize he'd better play his cards right tomorrow. She might not give him another chance if he blew it again.

He turned and headed toward the courtroom for his hearing. When he reached the door, he looked back. She appeared to be watching him go. When their eyes met, she smiled and then looked away as if embarrassed to have been caught. Yes, there was something special about her. Now if he could just figure out a way to get over what she did for a living.

21

SARAH

Months passed. When Sarah arrived for her scheduled visit, Anne pulled her aside. "Mrs. Thornton, I want to let you know from now on, you'll see each of your children separately. Thirty minutes each."

"What? Why?"

"Ryan is upsetting Leanna. It's best to separate them. They will be here shortly. I will bring them in one at a time." With that she exited the room.

Sarah felt like a boiler furnace lit up inside her. These were her children and yet, no one talked to her about the arrangements. Moments later, the door opened and Leanna entered. "Mommy, Mommy." She held up her arms.

Lifting her, Sarah realized Leanna wore a diaper. That was odd. Leanna potty trained early. She hadn't worn a diaper for over six months. Now she has a diaper again? With only thirty minutes, she didn't want to waste time fussing about it. They snuggled, played peek-a-boo, and read one of Leanna's favorite stories.

When the caseworker came for Leanna, she gave her mommy a quiet hug and took the lady's hand. In her free hand, she clutched her dolly's arm. As she walked away, her head dropped and her little feet made heavy thuds down the hall. Her dolly's legs dragged along. Sarah felt like she was crumbling as she watched her baby leave.

A few minutes passed and Ryan arrived. His shoulders were slumped and his face seemed to have aged beyond his almost eight years. He didn't make eye contact.

"Ryan, come give me a hug."

He walked the few steps to her and limply put one arm around her waist.

"Honey, are you okay?" She lifted his chin to look into his face.

His eyes were dark and sad. He remained silent.

"Son, has something happened?"

He averted his gaze to the mirror on the wall. He was a smart boy. He knew someone was watching them.

Sarah pulled him into a hug. "Son, you can tell me. Whisper it if you must."

Still, he hesitated. Then he turned his back to the mirror. He whispered in her ear. "Mom, there are mean boys where I live. I'm scared."

She felt a chill run down her spine. Her son was no longer under her protection. It didn't sound like he was under anyone's protection.

"Can you tell me what happened?"

He shook his head no. She persisted, but his jaw remained set.

A knock on the door jarred her from her focus on Ryan. She looked at her watch. Their visitation time wasn't up. Why were they being interrupted?

Anne opened the door. "It's time to say goodbye to your mom Ryan."

Ryan's eyes filled with tears. "Mama, please don't make me go back there. Please take me home. Please."

"I'm trying son."

"I want to come home with you NOW!" His tone changed from pleading to a desperate demand.

She took a step back. She'd never heard him talk like that. How could she explain to an eight-year-old the chaos of their lives? "Ryan, we love you. Daddy wanted me to tell you that he loves you too. He thinks of you every day."

Anne tapped the edge of the door frame with her fingernails. "Come along Ryan. Tell your mom goodbye."

Sarah stooped to look into his eyes. She gave him a hug. He returned the hug and hung on tight. She tried to loosen his hold, but didn't want him to feel pushed away. He let go. She kissed him on the forehead and smoothed his hair. Seeing his pain was enough to unravel her.

As he was led away, she watched while fighting tears. He turned around once to look at her and she blew him a kiss. When he was gone, she sat in a chair to gather her emotions. She felt raw. This issue of Ryan's fear needed to be addressed. Who could she talk to?

Looking down the hall, she saw Anne returning. Sarah motioned toward her. "I need to talk to you."

"And I need to speak with you." Anne came into the room and closed the door. "Mrs. Thornton, I must warn you. If the children continue to be upset with your visits, we will discontinue them."

Sarah clenched her fists and tried to control the fear that ripped through her. That must be why they cut the visit short, to show their threat was real. She fumbled with her purse, but it fell to the floor, spilling the contents. As she leaned to pick up her lipstick and billfold, she took a deep breath. She needed to remain calm. With everything shoved back in her purse, she stood and looked at Anne. She cleared her throat. "My son is scared. I don't think he's safe. Would someone please check on him?" Her voice shook.

"Oh, he's fine. He's probably overreacting since he has your attention." Anne leaned back against the closed door.

"No, I don't think he's fine. I need to get my children home."

Anne sighed. "We've been through this. That's not going to happen right now."

Sarah started to tremble. Ryan was scared. Leanna had regressed. She had to get her kids back yet, she feared if she said anything more, she might never see them again. She swallowed hard. "I need to get back to work."

Anne stepped aside and opened the door. Sarah walked past her and out the building without saying a word. She wanted to scream.

The state's requirements were ridiculous. This whole thing was ridiculous. Weekly meetings with caseworkers who told her how to behave. Visits with her children were manipulated. Required parenting classes. What a joke! She could teach those young instructors a thing or two about parenting. And the random drug tests, as if she'd ever used drugs! What choice did she have? She could either comply or risk losing her children. At the end of the day, her opinions, emotions, and feelings were irrelevant. All she could do was keep going and try her best to play by their rules.

22

SARAH

Tyler's trial date had been set. It would be over soon. Three days before jury selection, the judge delayed the trial citing personal reasons. Another delay followed. Each delay kept Tyler in jail and the children in foster care. Six months passed before jury selection began. That took two days. Finally, the trial began.

When Sarah walked into the courtroom, she was surprised to find it crowded. She made her way to a seat behind the rail that separated the courtroom from the defense table. Tyler was already there. She reached up and touched his back. He looked back at her and smiled. She smiled back. Inside she trembled.

The prosecutor presented his opening statement. "A young boy has died at the careless hands of his own father." She cringed as a murmur went through the crowd. "He was neglectful, reckless, and inattentive. What should have been a fun morning at the pool turned into tragedy due to this man's blatant disregard for the safety of his own child." Sarah gritted her teeth as the prosecutor continued. It was preposterous. Tyler adored his children and would give his life for them.

After opening statements, the prosecutor began calling a list of witnesses. He called forth people who had been at the pool that morning. He addressed the first witness. "Can you describe what you witnessed on the referenced day?"

"Yes, the guy just read a magazine. He wasn't even paying attention to that little guy."

Another testified, "I tried to strike up a conversation with him. Our kids were playing together. He seemed preoccupied."

As the witnesses gave their statements, none of them mentioned Tyler being there with three children, not just Noah. How could anyone have missed that? She wondered if the witnesses had even been at the pool that day.

The first long, torturous morning ended. When the court broke for lunch, Sarah followed the prosecutor out of the courtroom. Once in the hallway, she touched his arm, hoping to catch his attention. He turned and gave her a cool look.

"Sir, you're not describing my husband accurately. Anyone who knows him would testify he would never hurt his children."

"Someone is responsible for Noah's death. I'm surprised you wouldn't want justice for your son."

"How can justice be served if a loving father is accused of a crime that didn't happen? It was an accident, not a crime."

"I can't discuss this with you. You'll have an opportunity to present your side soon."

Tyler's attorney, Mr. Webber, caught up with her. He grasped her by the elbow and pulled her away. She turned to look at him. "How can you let him talk like that? Why aren't you objecting?"

"Calm down. I will do my best to defend Tyler when it's our turn, but you'll accomplish nothing if you're hysterical or confrontational, especially in front of the prosecutor."

She jerked her arm out of his grasp. "I'm not hysterical."

"Calm down."

"This is my husband's life. My family's life. You aren't defending him."

"You're not doing much for him either by ranting like this."

Her eyes widened into a harsh glare. How dare he speak to her like that! She turned and marched out of the courthouse. Once outside, she gulped in the air. She couldn't afford to be emotional. Too much was at stake.

The next day went even worse. The prosecutor called expert witnesses who described in great detail how frightening it was for a child to be submerged. They told of the pain of suffocation, implying Tyler had done that to Noah. Sarah sat shaking in her chair. The details of the trauma cut her to the core. Wasn't it bad enough that Noah died? To have to hear these details and the accusatory tones. She didn't know how much more she could take.

As the prosecutor continued to parade experts across the stand, Sarah noted their long list of credentials. Tyler's witnesses, his friends and family, could never sound as credible as these experts.

The prosecutor wasn't done. "I have one more document to present to the court."

She sighed. What more could he say that would make Tyler look worse than already portrayed?

"I am presenting into evidence a time sheet and disciplinary action Tyler's employer filed against him."

Sarah wracked her brain trying to figure out what he was talking about.

"As you can see, Tyler has a history of drunkenness. He failed to show up for work after a hangover. What kind of father can't stay out of the bar? Perhaps he had been drinking at the pool. That would explain things."

"Objection your honor. Speculation." Finally! Mr. Webber opened his mouth.

"Sustained. The jury will please disregard the last statement. Now continue."

"That's all your honor. The prosecution rests."

"Is the defense ready to begin?"

Mr. Webber stood. "Yes, your honor."

"Very well. Court will resume tomorrow and the defense will present its case. Court adjourned." The judge slammed down his hammer.

The guard escorted Tyler from the courtroom. Sarah felt too weary to move. As the courtroom cleared, Mr. Webber turned to her. "What do you know about that? Why didn't you tell me he has a drinking problem?"

"Because he doesn't."

He pulled out the document and showed it to her. She looked it over. "Oh, now I remember."

He rolled his eyes and slapped his hand on his thigh. "Great."

"No, it's not like that. We hadn't been married long. We didn't even have children yet. Look at the date; nine years ago. New Year's Day. Yes, Tyler drank too many beers that night. Many young men do on New Year's Eve, but that never happened again. He has worked in the same auto repair shop for the past eight years. I don't recall him missing even one day of work at that time. His employer will verify that."

Mr. Webber leaned back in his chair and crossed his arms. She squinted her eyes. "You do intend to call his employer to the stand, don't you?"

He leaned forward and wrinkled his brow. "I guess I will have to now."

"Now? You hadn't planned to call his boss as a character witness?"

"Listen. You need to relax." He stood and turned his back to her. He lifted his briefcase from the floor and loaded the files.

"Relax? How can I relax? It feels like we're losing." She stood and walked around so she could look him in the eyes. "Mr. Webber, are you going to help my husband?"

"Of course, but it would have been nice to have known about this drinking issue."

Sarah let out an exasperated sigh. "He doesn't have a drinking issue. Are you listening to me?"

She could see a muscle tighten in his jaw. "Listen, now that the prosecutor is done, we'll have our chance to clear things up."

"If it's not too late. Have you seen how the jury looks at Tyler? They've already convicted him. The truth isn't coming out! Tyler is a wonderful father and devoted husband. He works hard to provide for us. He loves us."

Mr. Webber raised himself up and pushed his shoulders back. "If you're unhappy with my services, I'm sure a new attorney can be appointed."

She bit her lip, doing her best to hold back her frustration. She wasn't happy with him but they couldn't get a new attorney at this point. "Let me take the stand."

"That's not a good idea."

She stepped back. "Why not?"

"Because you're too emotional. It won't come across well."

Sarah threw her hands up in the air. "I need to talk to Tyler. ALONE!"

"I'll arrange for that tomorrow. Tonight, I need to prepare." His curt and hard tone gave her notice he was done talking. He turned and walked away. She left in the opposite direction, muttering to herself all the way to the parking lot.

When she got home that night, she could hardly get out of the car. Her legs felt like they were weighed down in concrete. She walked up the sidewalk to the house. When she got to the door, she checked the mailbox. Nothing but bills. Glancing down, she noticed the flower bed. The weeds overtook the petunias. She felt as defeated as the flowers. She unlocked the door and let herself in. Other than the clicking sound from the second hand on the wall clock, silence filled the house. She never got used to this. She hoped it wouldn't be that way much longer. She turned on the radio. That helped to fill the void.

Food no longer tasted good, but she knew she needed to eat. She put a piece of bread in the toaster and peeled a hard-boiled egg. As she waited for the toaster to pop, she looked around the kitchen. Her children's art hung on the refrigerator. Their fingerprints were on the windows. Leanna's shoes were near the door that led to the backyard. They wouldn't even fit her anymore, but she refused to move anything, to change anything. Her family would come home to the same house they left. She grabbed a blanket and curled up in Tyler's well-used recliner. The cushion was a bit flat, but it was comfortable. It made her feel close to him. Like many other nights, she fell asleep there. The egg and toast never made it to her mouth.

23

SARAH

Sarah woke up early the next morning in the recliner. She rubbed her eyes and stretched. A hot shower would feel good after another restless night.

Arriving at the courthouse well ahead of schedule, she waited for Tyler. She hoped Mr. Webber arranged for them to talk as he promised. Relief swept over her when she saw Tyler being escorted in a little earlier than usual. They were given a few moments in a private room as the guard stood outside.

She sat in the chair next to Tyler and reached for his hand. Her words came out in a gush. "Tyler, I feel like we're losing. The jury hasn't been given a fair view of who you are."

"We'll get our turn today honey."

"Are you sure Mr. Webber is capable of representing you? I don't think he's giving your defense much effort." She didn't want to add to his worries, but she had to share her concerns. He squeezed her hand. "We have to trust he can do the job. He's worked hard preparing. Let's give him a chance."

She looked down at her lap. "I just wish we could have hired one of the attorneys George recommended."

"We've been over this Sarah. I don't want you working any more than you already are, and I refuse to take out a second mortgage to pay for this. No matter how this comes out, I want you and the kids to have a home."

"If we ever get them home." Her chin started to tremble.

Tyler took her face in his hands and pulled her chin up so he could look in her eyes. "Sarah. We will. We'll get through this." He kissed her.

A tear made its way down her cheek. "I hope so. I feel like we're outgunned. The prosecutor seems to have limitless time and an unending budget. It doesn't seem to bother him how long this drags out." She paused. "I can't afford to keep taking time off work."

Tyler reached to wipe her tears away. "I know honey. You're handling all this so well. I appreciate you so much. I'm so proud of you."

The compliment created a lump in her throat. Tears came more rapidly. "I'll bet that big shot prosecutor even gets to tuck his kids in at night." Her words came out in a hoarse whisper. Tyler pulled her into his arms. She wept into his shoulder.

A knock on the door startled them. "Court is about to reconvene."

Sarah reached for a Kleenex and wiped her eyes and blew her nose.

As Tyler was led from the room, he paused and turned to her. "Sarah, no matter what happens. If this doesn't end well..."

She wouldn't let him finish. "Tyler, you can't give up. We are going to fight this."

"I'm not giving up. It's just that, well, I'm not sure we can win this."

"Don't say that. I need you. We all need you."

He nodded.

The guard escorted Tyler to the courtroom. Sarah found a seat behind him. She glanced around the room. Reporters and strangers seemed to gawk. She felt out of place and misunderstood. The dark, dreary room left her feeling weary and discouraged.

As the court convened, Tyler's attorney began presenting his case. Sarah's fears grew as the prosecutor cross-examined each witness. It felt more like a witch hunt than an effort to bring forth the truth. She wondered if Tyler was right. Perhaps there was no way to win. Perhaps the past six months of fatigue began to cloud her judgment. Perhaps she no longer had a sense of reality. Nothing seemed certain anymore.

*　　*　　*　　*　　*

The first week concluded. Both sides presented their case. Closing comments would be on Monday. When Sarah arrived at the courtroom Monday morning, she braced herself for another long, agonizing day. As she took her seat behind Tyler, he didn't turn around to greet her as he normally did. Something was different. His shoulders were slumped. A blank stare filled his face. She wondered what changed.

The judge called the court to order and directed his attention to the prosecutor. "I understand you have reached a plea agreement?"

"Yes, your honor."

Sarah gasped. Tyler continued to look straight ahead. She cleared her throat and nudged Mr. Webber's chair. He didn't seem to notice. She looked around the room, looking for answers.

The judge looked at Tyler. "Is it your understanding you will forgo a jury verdict and instead, accept the terms of your plea agreement?"

Tyler nodded.

Sarah felt dizzy as she dug her fingernails into the arms of her chair.

The judge continued to address Tyler. "Could you please verbalize your response for the record?"

Tyler cleared his throat. "Yes, your honor. That is what I have agreed to." His words were flat.

The room started to spin. Sarah sucked in a deep breath and put her head in her hands. She couldn't pass out here.

"Very well." The judge turned his attention to the jury. "The jury may be dismissed. Thank you for your service to the court and our community." They stood and filed out of the courtroom. As they left, most of them cast accusing looks at Tyler.

After the jury left, the judge turned to look at Tyler. "As a result of your plea agreement, I hereby sentence you to twenty-five years in the state prison for negligent homicide and child endangerment. Court is adjourned." He slammed down the gavel and the courtroom burst into a sea of activity. Sarah covered her mouth with her hand as she attempted to stifle a scream.

The guards made their way to Tyler. He turned to look at her. She stood and rushed to him. The guard gave her a moment to embrace Tyler. "Why Tyler? Why?"

His chin trembled. "I'm sorry."

The guards led him away. She watched him leave as waves of nausea rolled through her body. She couldn't imagine anything worse than knowing Tyler would be in prison for the next twenty-five years.

That was only the beginning. Later that afternoon, when she arrived at the CPS office to visit her children, they weren't there. Anne informed her that when Tyler took the plea agreement, admitting neglect of his son, Sarah became guilty of not protecting the children from Tyler. Thus, with the drop of the judge's gavel, not only had Tyler been sentenced to prison, all parental rights were terminated. She never saw Ryan or Leanna again.

24

ASHLEY

The phone woke Ashley from a deep sleep. She felt disoriented as she glanced at the clock. Two a.m. Dread filled her mind. These nighttime calls were never good news. As she looked at the phone number display, she recognized the crisis call center. She was the "on call" caseworker. It happened more often since the department couldn't keep fully staffed. Caseworker burn-out caused high turnover and heavy caseloads.

"Sorry to wake you Ashley, but we have an emergency situation."

"No problem. What do you know so far?" She rubbed her eyes as she tried to force her mind to wake.

"The police are on scene at the Walmart parking lot. A woman passed out behind the wheel of her car. A passerby noticed two toddlers crying in the back seat."

"I'll be right there." She hung up the phone. These were the calls that made her angry. Thank goodness the woman parked her car before she passed out, otherwise, the call might have gone to the morgue.

Looking around, she realized she fell asleep on the sofa, completely clothed. She swung her feet to the floor and stretched her stiff body. The couch was not the best place to get a good night's rest. What day was it anyway? She remembered seeing RT. Was that yesterday? If so, did that mean they had a date tonight?

She staggered into the bathroom and splashed cold water on her face. This level of chaos had become second-nature. No time to ponder it now. She needed to get these little ones to safety.

She smoothed her wrinkled clothes with her hands, brushed her hair, and passed a toothbrush over her cotton-mouth teeth. Grabbing her car keys, she headed out. As she drove the short distance to Walmart, she prayed for the family. And she prayed for herself. These children had such hard lives. How could she complain about how rough her last twenty-four hours were compared to what these little ones endured on a daily basis?

When she pulled up next to the police car, she could see a woman sitting in the backseat of the patrol car. She looked asleep, or passed out. One policeman held a child who seemed intrigued with the officer's hat, as she kept taking it on and off the officer's head. Another toddler was still in the car seat. The other officer talked to her, holding a small teddy bear. How she appreciated these men and women in blue.

She knew both these officers from previous calls. She greeted them by name and listened to their report. Officer Todd gave her the details. "We received a call from a shopper who noticed the children crying. The mom was slumped over the wheel. She's drunk. Couldn't pass the sobriety test. Her driver's license says her name is Nichole Smith. We will book her on a DUI and child endangerment."

"Thank you so much for helping the children, Officer Todd. I'll get them into an emergency foster home tonight and open a case." She nodded toward the mom. "It doesn't look like I'll get much information from her tonight."

"No, I don't think so. She should sober up by morning. A night in jail tends to do that."

"I'll stop by in the morning to visit with her then."

"Thanks Ashley. I'll be sure to let the front desk know you'll be by."

She moved the toddler from the car seat in Nicole's car and buckled her into the car seat in her own car. Officer Todd buckled up the older girl. Both children were quiet as they waited in her backseat. She took a moment to contact her emergency foster home, letting them know she was in route. Both children were fast asleep when she pulled up to the home.

The foster mom, Kim stood on the porch waiting for her. She smiled even as she stood in her bathrobe under the porch light with rumpled hair. She met Ashley at the car and together they unloaded the sleepy girls and tucked them into beds. Neither child stirred.

"Thank you so much," Ashley whispered.

"Oh, I love doing this."

"You have a great attitude considering I woke you up in the middle of the night." Ashley smiled.

"I'm glad I could help."

They moved from the bedrooms to the living room. Ashley touched Kim's arm. "You can't imagine how important you are to us. It would be a pretty uncomfortable night in my office if you weren't willing to take them on such short notice." Ashley felt the need to apologize. "I don't know much about the girls. I don't even know their names. I'll learn more tomorrow. I'll keep you posted."

"Sounds great. Get some rest."

"You too. Thanks again Kim. You're a lifesaver." Ashley got in her car and headed to her apartment.

Back home, she unlocked her door and tossed her keys on the counter. Although her alarm wouldn't go off for another hour, she wouldn't be able to sleep. Her mind buzzed, thinking of the tasks ahead. A shower would help revitalize her. Clean clothes would help too.

Standing in the steamy water, she thought of the many other times she'd rescued children from the cars of drunk drivers. Most parents who struggled with addictions weren't bad people. They just made bad choices. Sometimes, with the right help, they could learn to make better choices, but not unless they were ready. She wondered what state of mind this woman would be in.

After making a fruit smoothie, she headed to the office. She needed to get this case opened and visit the mom in jail. Perhaps the police gathered more information in the last few hours.

At the office she entered the case into her computer and headed for the jail. She showed her identification and followed the staff to a briefing room. It contained a sterile steel table and two chairs. She sat in one of them. A few minutes later, Nichole came into the room with a police officer. Her eyes met Ashley's for a brief moment before diverting them to the floor. She took a seat and the officer left the room.

"Hi Nichole. I'm Ashley. I'm with Child Protective Services. I took your children to a foster home last night."

She looked up. "Are they okay?"

"Yes, they are fine."

"I can't believe I put my children in danger." Tears were brimming in her eyes. "I love them so much."

"I'm sure you do. Can you tell me what happened?" Ashley wanted to give her the benefit of the doubt.

Nichole nodded, but didn't speak for a moment. "I've been going through a bad spell lately." She quickly added, "I've been sober for five years."

"So, you've struggled with addictions before?"

"Yes." Her eyes returned to the table while her legs fidgeted.

"Can you tell me more?" Nichole didn't look up. She didn't answer.

Ashley wanted her to feel comfortable in sharing with her. "It's okay Nichole, I'm here to help."

Nichole pulled on a loose strand of hair as her eyes shifted between Ashley and the table. When she spoke, her words came out in a slow whisper. "I started drinking in my teens, but I got straightened out. Got in a program. Like I said, I've been sober for five years."

"You've had a bad spell?

She chewed on her hair and nodded. Her eyes met Ashley's. She hesitated before answering. "Yes, my boyfriend left me."

"I'm sorry. Do you have any family in town? Anyone who can support you during this time?"

"No, it's just me and my kids. May I see them? Please?"

"We will get to that, but for now, we need to get you some help. You put yourself and your children in extreme danger last night."

"I know. I'll never do that again."

What a relief to hear her acknowledge her mistake. A good first step, but she needed to do more than acknowledge it. Ashley cleared her throat. "Unfortunately, due to the severity of the situation, we need to be sure they will be safe before we can return them to you."

"Oh, they will be. I promise. I will never do that again."

"I'm sure you don't intend to Nichole, but there is a process. Do you understand you'll need to start over with your sobriety? That you'll need to get counseling and attend meetings?"

"Whatever I have to do to get them back." Her words were pleading.

Ashley let silence fill the room for a bit. "I know you want them back, but when that happens is up to you. We'll need to do frequent urine analysis tests, or UA's, to confirm you're staying sober."

Nichole nodded.

"This won't be easy, but if you are willing, I will help you." Nichole needed to understand she had a lot of work to do before she could get her children back. No amount of counseling, meetings, or treatment plans would "fix" someone unless they wanted the help and wanted to make changes.

Nichole continued to nod.

"Okay, I'll put a treatment and parenting plan together for you."

As Ashley left the jail house, her shoulders felt heavy. Time seemed to be going in slow motion. Lack of sleep had taken its toll. Her thoughts were still on Nichole. She seemed sincere, but once parents lose their children, they often lose hope. As a result, they lose their motivation to stay sober, and relapse into their addiction.

She wondered what happened to Nichole that caused her to turn to alcohol to begin with, before her boyfriend's actions caused her to relapse. Mental illness, past traumas. It could be a number of things. Perhaps she had been a foster child. It wasn't unusual for generations to repeat cycles of abuse, trauma, and addictions. She groaned. It wasn't even 9:00 a.m. and she was on fumes. She couldn't get her mind off Nichole. Ashley hoped she would take advantage of the services offered to her. Her kids needed her to be a healthy mom.

25

ASHLEY

Ashley felt like the walking dead. Her day started fifteen hours ago when she rescued two children from their mother's car at Walmart. There hadn't been a break all day and now, she had a half hour to get to the restaurant to meet RT. She would have preferred to cancel, but with no way to contact him, she had to go. It would be rude to not show up.

She popped into the lady's room at work and attempted to freshen up. Slapping cool water on her face, her skin tingled. She applied a light layer of foundation and lipstick. Viewing herself in the mirror, she acknowledged she looked a bit better, even if she didn't feel it. Regardless, this was as good as it was going to get.

As she drove into the parking lot of the restaurant, she noticed RT. He pulled in just ahead of her. She watched as he exited his car. He shed the business suit and wore crisp jeans and a polo shirt. At the sight of his clean look, she felt haggard. How she wished she could have made a trip home, taken a shower, and put on fresh clothes, but she was here now. She hoped she could pull the evening off with the fatigue she felt.

When she entered the restaurant, she noticed him standing inside the door. He greeted her with a wide grin and gave her a tender hug. Wow, that helped to renew her. As the waitress led them to a table, she felt a bit giddy. Having dinner with him might be just what she needed.

He started the conversation. "So, how was your day?"
"Very long..."

"Care to share?"

She nodded her head emphatically. "No. I'd really like to forget it and focus on something else."

He smiled. "Fair enough. Would you like to start with a drink?"

"Sure, I'd love a glass of wine."

He opened the wine list. He seemed unsure as he flipped back and forth. He ordered a beer along with her Riesling.

Eager to put the heaviness of the day behind her, Ashley picked up the conversation. "So how many bad guys did you defend this week?" She smirked as the question came off in a playful tone.

He seemed to take it in stride. "Hey, I only defend the innocent."

"Ya, ya. You defense attorneys all say that."

He seemed to enjoy the banter although he didn't respond.

"So how did you get into this gig anyway?" She really did want to know.

He dropped his eyes. His smile faded. "I hoped to get to know you a little better before delving into that. I owe you an explanation for my reaction last time we met. Are you sure you want to know?"

Seeing the change in his demeanor, she wished she hadn't asked, but she couldn't say no now.

He looked across the room as if searching for someone. Her curiosity grew. He looked back at her and took a deep breath. "I was a foster kid."

She hadn't expected that. She leaned forward and put her hand over his, giving it a squeeze, then pulled it away, not wanting it to linger. "Please. Continue."

"It wasn't a good experience. I started out in a group home. There were ten of us sharing four twin beds. I went to other group homes after that. Eventually I ended up in a nice foster home. They cared for me and even went to the effort of adopting me."

She knew this conversation could trigger unwanted memories. She didn't want him to feel pressured to talk, but this was intriguing. "Wow. You don't have to talk about this if you don't want to."

"No, it's okay. I've talked about it a lot. It is what it is."

"If you're sure."

He nodded.

"So, how old were you when you were adopted?"

"Ten. It didn't end well."

She proceeded with caution. "What happened?"

"I didn't want to be adopted. I just wanted to go home. I made it hard for them. A few years after the adoption was finalized, I ran away. When they found me on the streets, they put me in a foster home, then a group home, followed by another, and another." His gaze shifted to the walls.

"Oh, my goodness." Ashley took a sip of wine, giving him time to decide how much more he wanted to share. She noticed the waitress coming their way. They should order their food. She picked up the menu. He did the same.

The waitress introduced herself as Brandi and started chatting about the weather. Ashley wanted to get back to her conversation with RT. She didn't want to be rude, so she pointed to the menu and made her selection. RT ordered as well. They both shut their menus and handed them to Brandi. She didn't take her cue as she rambled on about the upcoming Seahawks game. Ashley noticed most of Brandi's words were directed at RT. It seemed flirtatious, but RT appeared oblivious.

Ashley cleared her throat. "Thank you for taking our order. You've been very helpful." She looked at Ashley as if she'd just noticed her. Brandi nodded and left to put their orders in with the chef. Ashley redirected her eyes to RT. He rubbed the back of his neck. A sad look crept into his eyes.

"Please continue. You said you were in a lot of group homes?"

He nodded his head. "Yes, eight to be exact. Each time I got meaner because I had to be tougher than the kids from the last home who beat me up, or pinned me to the wall, or tried to suffocate me."

Her hand flew up to cover her mouth. "How awful. Did you try to get help, or tell someone?"

"When the caseworker came to check on me, most of the time my abusers were right there, so I couldn't say anything. A few times I tried, but I always paid for it. I learned to keep my mouth shut."

Ashley could feel tears in her eyes. "That's so hard for me to understand. I would never leave a child in a situation where they were in danger." Her voice quivered.

"You are obviously better than the caseworkers I had."

"I'm so sorry."

"No, it's okay. I survived, right?" He smiled, but it didn't last long.

"Were all the homes bad?" She hoped to hear something positive.

"Not all of them, but most of them. In those, we foster kids were just a number. In one of the homes, our foster parents beat us, and then joked they had to keep us alive so they could collect their monthly stipend."

She'd heard rumors of foster homes like that, but couldn't bring herself to believe they really existed.

"Most of my caseworkers were women. They didn't seem to care about my safety. I think that's why I reacted the way I did the other night. I guess I still have issues..." He looked away as his voice trailed off.

"I am so very sorry R. T."

"Don't apologize. You didn't do any of it. I'm actually relieved to meet a caseworker who seems genuine. I wish someone like you had been helping me back then." His gaze intensified.

She gulped and then smiled. She had so many questions, but remained quiet, giving him time to continue.

Just then chatty Brandi came back with their food. Again, she remained longer than necessary as she tried to engage in conversation with RT. Just when Ashley thought she would need to say something, Brandi noticed her boss signaling her. She scurried off with the promise to return for the dessert order.

Ashley looked at RT and rolled her eyes. "Please continue. Goodness, how many times have I said that?"

He gave her a coy smile. "Anyway, my last group home was the end of the line for kids like me. I decided the only way out was to join the military, so the moment I turned eighteen, I joined."

"Seriously?" She couldn't believe it. She would never have believed this sharp, put-together attorney had been a former foster kid, let alone ex-military.

"Yes. The few, the proud, the Marines!" A smile crossed his face. She returned it with one of her own, but inside her heart felt like lead sinking to the bottom of a pool. He was one of those children who never had a family, one who hadn't been rescued soon enough. Would there ever be an end to hurting children, or parents who caused such suffering? She looked down at her hands.

He reached over and took one of her hands in his. "Hey, enough about me. Let's talk about you."

Ashley wanted to hear more. She hoped he would continue. "No, I want you to finish. What happened next? How did you go from being a Marine to an attorney?"

He hesitated. His lips pinched together. "I went to boot camp, likely the best thing that happened to me. My drill sergeant worked my bad attitude out of me. I can't tell you how many pushups and laps he made me do, just to knock the huge chip off my shoulder. I'm pretty sure my fellow recruits didn't appreciate the extras they were forced to do on my account."

A smile crossed her face as she thought of him having to do extra pushups.

"Quite the visual, huh?"

"No, it's not that. I just can't imagine you as a rebellious Marine with a bad attitude."

"Trust me. I was, but my sergeant took an interest in me. I think I reminded him of himself at an earlier time."

"Really?

He nodded and cleared his throat. "Yes. He told me to get an education. So, whenever I could, I took online courses. I used my GI bill to go to law school. I realized with my stubborn streak, I just might make a good attorney. I love a good argument."

"So, I've noticed." She laughed.

He leaned his elbow on the table and put his face closer to hers. "Oh, you have no idea. You really should come watch me defend the innocent sometime!"

"If you ever get an innocent client, I just might." She raised her eyebrows.

RT smiled and winked. "I'm going to hold you to it."

Just then a yawn escaped Ashley. She covered her mouth to try to hide it.

RT leaned back in his chair. "I'm sorry. This must have been so boring."

"No, no, not at all. It's been a long day. It started out twenty hours ago when I rescued two little girls from the Walmart parking lot."

RT's mouth dropped open. "Are you kidding me? Why didn't you say something?"

"What? And miss this conversation? Not for the world, but as much as I've enjoyed this, I should get home."

They both rose. RT opened his wallet and left enough money under the napkin to cover the bill. "My treat!" he stated, as Ashley reached for her purse.

They took a couple steps when Brandi returned. "What, no dessert?" A pout, complete with pursed lips, covered her face.

RT smiled. "No. Not tonight." Without warning, he scooped Ashley into his arms. She felt her face flush. He turned his face toward hers, bringing it only inches away and lowered his voice.

"We've got another dessert planned." Keeping her close to his side, they walked toward the door.

Ashley stifled a giggle. Once outside, she pulled away and burst out laughing. "R. T.! You are so bad."

He bowed and then doubled over as he joined in her laughter. It took him a moment to catch his breath. His words came out between fits of laughter. "I thought I needed to let Brandi down slowly."

"So, you noticed her flirting?"

"Of course. It happens all the time." He waved his hand, mocking humility.

"I have no doubt about that." She burst out laughing again.

They continued their banter as he walked her to her car. Once they reached her car door, the smile slipped from his face as he took her hand. "No, not really. I was already with the prettiest girl tonight."

Ashley felt her face heating into a blush. Hopefully RT wouldn't notice in the dark parking lot. She squeezed his hand. "Thank you so much. I've really enjoyed our evening."

"Me too. Let's do this again."

She nodded. "I'd like that."

"Goodnight." He returned the squeeze and turned to walk to his car.

As Ashley drove back to her apartment, she giggled thinking again about their exit. Their conversation swirled in her mind. How interesting that he too had been a foster child. At another time, it would be fun to share her story. Then again, her life had been so different from his. It might seem like rubbing salt in his wounds.

Thoughts of how he had been mistreated by foster parents, in group homes, even by caseworkers, made her shudder. No wonder he was leery of her when she told him of her profession.

She wondered what happened that caused him to be taken from his biological family. That same question haunted her about her own family. Why did she keep putting it off? Guilt? Worry that it would hurt her mom? Maybe fear? Or maybe the time had come to stop making excuses and try to see what she could learn.

When she crawled into her bed, it felt so good. Her thoughts returned to him. A smile tugged at her lips. He was obviously intelligent, and witty. Her dad would have liked him. She felt a catch in her throat as thoughts of her dad came to mind. Oh, how she missed him. How she would have loved for him to meet RT, but this relationship hadn't gotten to the point of introducing him to her parents. Not yet. Perhaps it never would. Sure, there had been some flirting, but it seemed more friendly than romantic. Then again, she'd been the one who set the tone by accusing him of defending the guilty, pitting her profession against his. How would there ever be romance if she made this into a sparring contest? Oh brother, would she ever get this dating thing right?

26

ASHLEY

When Ashley arrived at the office the next morning, her co-worker James hovered near her office. "Hey, you got a minute?"

"Always for you." Ashley smiled. James had only been around for about six months. They worked on a number of cases together. She mentored him in the first months and he often conferred with her on his cases. She liked him as a professional. He had a fresh, honest desire to help the kids, just as she did when she started five years ago. He still had the energy and the 'I can change the world' attitude. She used to have it too, but in recent months, she felt weary. Perhaps she was still grieving her dad's death. It might be her new supervisor, or maybe she needed to get into a different line of work. This job was taking a toll.

As James took a seat in her office, he sat with a heavy thud and let out a sigh. He nudged the door shut with his foot. "I don't think I'm cut out for this job." Not a surprising comment for a newer caseworker, but she had such high hopes he would be one of those who could hang in there for at least a few years.

"One of my foster children died last night."

"What? What happened?" A chill ran down her spine.

James remained quiet. His hands were shaking. "It's my fault."

"Oh James, why would you say that?"

"No, it really is. Last time while at the foster home, I felt uneasy. I should have looked around more, stayed there to just make sure everything was okay. You know how it is. We can't stay too long at any location. With over forty cases, there are too many kids to check on."

She waited for him to continue. He took a deep breath. "Anyway, I guess they had a meth lab there. The house burned down last night and our child was left inside." He buried his face in his hands. His shoulders started shaking.

Ashley moved around the desk to put her hand on his shoulder. "How could you have known?"

He took some time to gather himself. "I couldn't have, but I should have. The foster home was licensed. I assumed it was okay. The parents seemed nice, like they cared for the kids, but it was still my responsibility. I should have checked more carefully on the safety of that little guy." His eyes were downcast.

She didn't know what to say. They trained for so many scenarios, but this wasn't one of them. How do you tell biological parents, who have been forced to relinquish their child due to neglect or abuse, that their child died in a home even more dangerous than their own?

"It looks like the foster parents will be charged. They were arrested earlier this morning." He let out a sigh. "This is a nightmare!"

Grief hung in the air. No matter how hard they tried to protect children, they couldn't in every situation. Life had its cruel moments, and this was one of them.

"James, you can't blame yourself. This is a horrible tragedy. We are all doing the best we can, under the circumstances."

He shook his head and rose, looking like a tired, arthritic old man. "That might be true, but it's not enough. I can't do this job Ashley. I just can't do it." He stood and walked out of her office. That afternoon, he resigned.

27

SARAH

Sarah almost couldn't bear the shock of losing the children. The only thing she had left was Tyler, even if he was in jail. So, when he could have visitors, she made the trek to the state prison to see him. She had to talk to him.

A month had passed since the trial. They hadn't been allowed to speak in that time. As she waited to be cleared to enter the visitation room, she picked at her nails. After being escorted in, she took a seat in a cubicle and waited. What a miserable place. Scratched safety glass separated the visitors from the inmates. Pea green paint peeled from the wall. A filthy black phone hung in the cubicle. She wished she could wipe it clean before she touched it. She shook her head. She had more important matters.

When he entered, she wasn't ready for what she saw. Tyler had a black eye. It had started to turn yellow. She covered her mouth with her hand as her eyes popped wide. He glanced at her, then looked into his lap before raising his eyes to meet hers. He picked up the phone hanging on his side of the glass. She did the same.

"What happened?"

He cleared his throat. "Honey, I know it looks bad, but I'm okay. Just a little 'get acquainted' ritual." He smiled, then pinched his lips together to try to hide the gaping hole where his front teeth had once been.

She gasped. "What happened to your teeth?" She could feel tears welling in her eyes.

"It's okay. I'll get through this." He paused. "How are you holding up?"

"Okay." It came out in a squeak.

"You look so beautiful." He smiled again, then clamped his mouth shut. He looked down again. "I'm so sorry Sarah. I had no idea that would happen to the kids."

She looked away. Anger rushed at her like a freight train out of control. She looked back at him and took a deep breath before responding. "Why did you take the plea agreement? Why didn't you talk to me first?" Her voice shook.

"I couldn't watch you go through it anymore. I could see how exhausted you were. I thought if I got out of the way, the kids would be free to come home. Never in my wildest..." He couldn't complete the sentence.

She stared at him for a while. As angry as she felt, the only thing she wanted to do was hold him, to be held by him, and get lost in his strong arms. She couldn't imagine the guilt he must be feeling over what his decision had cost them.

"Have you heard anything?" His question sounded tentative, as if afraid to ask.

She shook her head. Her throat tightened with emotion as tears spilled down her face. They sat in silence for a while.

"Sarah, if I could do it over." He gasped. "I would never let this happen to you."

"I know." She attempted to wipe away tears, but they kept flowing.

"Will you ever be able to forgive me?"

She sat motionless; her head bowed toward her chest as it heaved. Her mind swirled with emotion as she tried to piece together all the turmoil, and find some order in life. She needed time to heal, but she didn't want him to suffer further. He would never forgive himself for Noah's death, let alone this. She couldn't leave him thinking she wouldn't forgive him. "Tyler, I promised to love you forever. I intend to keep that promise. Forgiving you is part of loving you."

He choked, holding back a sob. They sat in silence for a long time. Before long, it was time to go. She put her hand on the glass. His hand matched hers on the other side.

"I love you, Tyler. I will always love you."

*   *   *   *   *

As the years passed, Sarah counted down the time in weeks. Every Sunday meant visitation day at the prison. Every Sunday she got to see him. It's not how she planned to spend her Sundays, but he's all she had. Two years down. Twenty-three more to go.

She glanced at her watch and realized she needed to get on the road. Pulling back her long brown hair, she gave herself a quick look in the mirror. As she drove to the prison, she thought of what they should be doing. They should be in church with their children. They should be enjoying a meal, playing board games, or napping. They should be together.

At the gate, the guards greeted her. She went through the process of emptying her pockets and going through the security screening. She was a familiar face to them now. She brought them fresh cookies once in a while. It couldn't hurt to do something kind for them. It might make Tyler's life a little better.

In the visitation room, she sat in the chair and looked through the thick glass, tapping her foot. This is what her life had come to, seeing Tyler for one hour every week. Her heart skipped a beat when he approached the glass. He smiled. Oh, how she loved his smile, especially since his front teeth had been replaced. She'd paid for false ones, knowing it would make him feel better. Picking up the phones, they greeted one another.

She spoke first. "You look good." His clean-shaven face looked so handsome.

"Not near as good as you. You're a sight for sore eyes."

They talked of her work and his new responsibilities at the prison. The conversation lulled.

"You know, I was thinking about when we first met." Tyler's eyes sparkled as if sharing a secret.

"What made you think of that?"

"Oh, I don't know. You are all I ever think about. It helps to pass the time and makes me think of happier times."

She smiled. "So, what about when we first met?"

"For starters, you took the air out of my lungs. You were the most beautiful girl I'd ever seen. You still are."

"And you're still a flirt." She smiled.

Tyler winked. "Only when it comes to you my love, but you sure didn't make it easy on me. Do you remember how many times I asked you out before you agreed?"

"Three. I was shy. Plus, you had me in nervous knots just looking at your big muscles."

They laughed. It felt good to laugh. It had been a long time.

"I remember stealing that first kiss in front of your parents' house. I knew right then you'd be the only girl I'd ever kiss."

She sighed. "Yes, and how angry our parents were when we eloped. We thought we were so wise at eighteen. We had everything figured out, until Ryan came along."

He chuckled. "No kidding. He changed our perspective. Thank goodness for him. I don't think our folks would have ever forgiven us had it not been for him. Giving them a grandchild seemed to cover for earlier blunders."

A tear escaped her eye. She dug into her purse and pulled out a tissue.

"I'm sorry honey. I miss the kids so much." He would never get over the fact he was responsible.

She cleared her throat and nodded. "Me too. We still have each other. We have wonderful memories." As hard as it was for her, it had to be even harder for him. She had to help him get through this.

He stared out into the distance and then looked at her. "Yes, we do." Then the corner of his mouth lifted. "You know what my favorite memory is?"

"What?"

"Camping. We were so broke. Yet, I felt like the richest man in the world sleeping on the ground with Ryan snuggled between us."

"Those were wonderful simple times. I sure couldn't cook over that campfire though. I think I burned everything." She chuckled.

"All I remember is the glow of your face as the campfire reflected off it." He caught his breath.

"You, my handsome husband, have always been my champion. Thank you for overlooking my flaws."

"No flaws. Just beauty." He paused. "I loved watching you tuck the children in at night. An incredible peace settled over the house as you read them bedtime stories and sang them to sleep. You were a wonderful mother."

"And you were a wonderful father."

Their time passed quickly. They said their goodbyes. When she walked to her car, her eyes were sore from holding back tears. Walking down memory lane had been so nice, but painful at the same time. She hoped someday, they could make new memories together.

28

TYLER

Sarah continued to come see Tyler every Sunday. She'd been coming for three years now and every time she came, he felt a gnawing in his heart. He felt selfish to expect her to wait for him. It wasn't fair that her life was on hold just because his was. He knew it was time to let her go. She would be coming tomorrow. He'd lain awake most of the night. When morning arrived, he still didn't know how to tell her.

When he got to the visitation room, he caught his breath at the sight of her. The pink ribbon in her hair matched the soft pink blouse she wore. Her fresh lipstick reminded him his lips would not touch hers, not with the thick glass wall separating them.

She picked up the phone hanging on the wall. He did the same.

"Hey beautiful."

She smiled. "How's it going?"

"The food's not as good as yours." He'd hoped it would earn him one of those smiles that caused his heart to quiver. It worked. He felt the familiar charge go through his body. Oh, how he longed to pull his wife into his arms, to soak up her warmth, and inhale the sweet scent of her hair. It was time to put that life behind him. She deserved more.

After some small talk, he decided it was now or never. There was so little to talk about anyway. He needed to get this over. "You know, I will always love you, Sarah."

"I will always love you too."

"Honey, I need to tell you something." He exhaled a deep breath. "I can't ask you to wait for me."

"You haven't. I am willing."

"No, please, let me say this." He raised his hand and sucked in a hard breath. "This is the hardest thing I'll ever say, but I have to." He took another breath to brace himself and pushed his words out in halted gasps. "Our time is over. You need to move on."

"No, Tyler, No."

"You deserve a new life. You're still young. I'll be an old man by the time I'm out. You are such a wonderful wife and mom. I want you to be that again."

She shook her head. Her lips trembled as tears rolled down her face. "No, don't do this."

He continued. "You were always my dream. You are my life; the very best thing in my life." He choked and took another breath. "I can't give you anything in return. I've thought about this. This is best." It broke him to see her so distraught. He would give anything to hold her, to comfort her, but he couldn't. That was the point. He couldn't do anything for her.

"No please, Tyler, don't. Don't give up on us." Her hands reached for him, but slammed into the glass.

"Honey, I would never give up on us, but there isn't an us anymore."

"Yes…there…is." Her words came out in jagged sobs.

"No, Sarah. All that is left is this horrible nightmare. It won't end. Not unless you move on." His jaw tightened as his resolve intensified. He had to get through this no matter how much it tore him apart, to finish this. "It's time for you to find a new love, and live a happy life. Go and light up the world the way you did mine. You deserve so much more than I can give you."

She clutched her phone and rose to her feet. "Tyler, please stop. Don't do this."

The guard approached her. "Ma'am, you must calm down or I'm going to have to ask you to leave." She glanced at him, but turned back to face Tyler.

"Ma'am..." The guard touched her shoulder. She jerked away.

Tyler knew she would get kicked out if this went on any longer. This had to end. He kissed his hand and pressed it to the glass. "Please, Sarah, don't come back. If you do, I won't come to see you. I will always love you, but you must go. This is my life now. You still have yours. Go live your life for all of us. Please, my love. Please."

He stood and put the phone on the receiver cradle. Turning his back, he walked away. He could hear his beautiful Sarah screaming. "STOP! Tyler Stop." He never looked back. He knew if he did, he would never let her go.

*   *   *   *   *

Every Sunday for the next two years, the guards tapped on Tyler's cell. "You've got a visitor. Your wife again."

"I'll stay here. Same as last week." He muttered to himself under his breath. "When will she give up?" Every time she came, it reminded him of what he lost. It refreshed his pain in saying goodbye

Months passed. The guards brought a thick envelope to him. He didn't recognize the return address. It had already been opened by prison security so the contents slipped out. Sheets of papers landed in his hand. As he unfolded them, a chill went through him. They were divorce papers.

His hands started to shake. This is what he wanted her to do, but deep down, it caught him by surprise. She was a strong-willed, tenacious woman. And stubborn. Hadn't she proved that by her continued visits? She knew how to hold her ground. That was part of the reason he loved her so much. In fact, when he stopped to think about it, had he ever won an argument with her? It looked like he had now.

He took a moment to glance over the ten-page packet. This was best. He had no right to her, not anymore. Besides, he wasn't the same person he once was. Life dealt its unfair blows and prison hardened him. He wasn't the man she once loved.

His hands were sweaty as he held the crisp paper. He stood to rap on his cell door. "Guard, I need a pen." Moments later, the guard brought one and stood over him, watching him. The pen felt like it weighed three pounds as he touched it to the paper. With each curve of his signature, the air in his body felt as if it was leaving. His hands shook as he folded the papers, put them back in the envelope, and handed them back to the guard, along with the pen.

He sat back on his cot, leaned his elbows on his knees, and stared at the floor. So, she'd finally decided to move on. Good for her. His life would never amount to anything beyond this prison anyway. It felt like a tourniquet wrapped itself around his heart.

* * * * *

Screams jolted Tyler awake as he sat upright in bed, soaked in sweat. His body trembled with memories of another nightmare. After losing everything in his life, they were the only thing that remained, continuing like the annoyance of a dripping faucet in the middle of the night.

He was with Noah. They were playing in the sand, making a sand castle.

"Daddy, Daddy, look! My castle!"

"It's amazing, son. You might make a good builder someday."

Noah nodded an enthusiastic yes.

He leaned down on the sand. "Tell me what you've made."

Noah pointed to a ditch in the sand. "A moat."

"Wow, son. I like it."

Noah flashed him a smile.

Out of nowhere, a wave crashed onto the sand and snatched Noah from the beach. Tyler chased the wave to the ocean, straining to save Noah. He could hear his son screaming, "Help Daddy. HELP!" His son's screams were in his dream, but in reality, Tyler's own screams awakened him.

Swinging his legs to the side of the bed, Tyler sat on the edge. He rubbed his eyes and shook his head, trying to empty his mind of the nightmare still frozen in his memory. A chill ran through him as his sweat soaked t-shirt grew cold in the night air. Groaning, he wondered if they would ever stop. Every nightmare started out differently, with a fun activity with Noah, but they all ended the same. His son died. Each time, he was reminded, he hadn't been able to save his own child.

29

SARAH

Sarah watched the children playing in their yard across the street. Their antics were so cute as they attempted to shoot a basket. "Pass it here Tommy. Pass it!" Their voices echoed across the driveway. Scuffling feet and grunts followed. Whoosh. "Score!" Cheers followed.

She loved to watch the children and yet it pained her too. They reminded her of the children she hadn't been allowed to watch grow up. Nearly twenty-five years passed since she'd last seen Ryan and Leanna. To this day, she didn't know what happened to them.

Turning away from the window, she once again wished she sold her house when the young family moved in, but selling her home wasn't an option. This is where the limited memories of her family still resided. It was her and Tyler's dream, a place to raise their family, even though that's not how it turned out.

She could remember the day she and Tyler brought Leanna home from the hospital. Ryan greeted them at the door. "Oh, Mommy. Let me hold her!" The two of them shared a closeness from then on. Although it wasn't the baby brother he wished for, he was a big brother all the same.

His wish for a little brother came a year later when Noah arrived. With the five-year age gap between Ryan and the two younger children, he was a wonderful helper. Thank goodness. With two little ones in diapers, Sarah needed all the help she could get. He was willing to grab a diaper, teach one of his siblings how to climb stairs, or just roll a ball on the floor with them.

She remembered how Leanna got stuck behind the china hutch while playing hide and seek, and how Noah managed to get himself on top of the counter by strategically climbing the kitchen drawers. She remembered the giggles. It made her smile just thinking of them. Being a mother had been her greatest joy.

She sighed as she jammed her hands into her pockets and wandered over to the phone to check for messages. It had become a habit even if the phone hadn't rung. She hardly ever used her landline now that she had a cell phone, but twenty-five years ago, when Ryan started school, she taught him how to spell his name, his address, and his phone number, this phone number. He wouldn't have forgotten it, would he? Yet, if he still remembered, why hadn't he called by now? Why hadn't he searched?

The "ifs" rolled through her mind. If she could have just said goodbye. If she could have known what happened to them. If she had gone to the pool, maybe none of this would have happened, but she couldn't roll back the time nor change the results. She wondered if they had been scared, or if they had been loved. Her children had been snatched from her life, kidnapped, in every sense. Left with the abyss of the unknown filled with "ifs", all she could do was pray.

Then again, who was she kidding? She wasn't sure prayer mattered. Her prayers hadn't worked when she'd begged for their return. Now it was too late. Her opportunity to be their mother, to raise, and to nurture them; gone. Even if they were alive, they were no longer children. Yet, just in case prayer really did make a difference, she continued to pray for them.

Tyler, now he was a different story. She was sure prayer wouldn't help him at all. What a hard-headed man. He had been her light, her love, her everything. She would have waited an eternity for him. He'd broken her heart by pushing her away. Still, she loved him. She tried to show him by continuing to come see him, but he never joined her in the visitation room again.

That's when she came up with the idea of having the divorce papers drawn up. She hoped it would knock some sense into him. To scare him into realizing no matter what, they belonged together. Instead, he'd signed the papers as if their marriage no longer mattered, as if she no longer mattered. She would never forget the sting she felt when the papers were delivered back to her so promptly.

She never filed them though. They were still in her desk, tucked away. She could never divorce him. No matter what he decided, she would love that hard-headed, stubborn man forever. No one else could share the memories of her children. No one else could know the pain of sitting at Noah's gravesite. No one else could understand the journey they endured. So even though he let their love go, she never would. She would wait, and if by some miracle Tyler or the children ever wanted to find her, this is where she would be, waiting for them. For that reason, she never sold the house.

30

TYLER

Tyler had seen many prisoners come and go through the decades he'd been in prison. His last cellmate had been released last week so it didn't surprise him when a new guy arrived in his cell. He looked to be in his mid-thirties. Nice looking kid. Clean cut. Sort of reminded him of himself when he first arrived.

He always felt sorry for the new guys. He remembered his first few months. He'd been mocked and jeered by the other prisoners. He'd missed more than one meal after it had been stolen. That wasn't the worst part. Convicted child killers aren't treated well, and if the other prisoners weren't bad enough, the guards did their part to make sure you didn't forget why you were here.

As he watched his new cell mate shuffle into the small space they would share, he pitied him. The kid had no idea what laid ahead. Rumor had it he'd been charged with child abuse and claimed to be innocent. Yah, just like every other prisoner here. As far as he could tell, in this place, he was the only one truly innocent.

Tyler nodded a greeting at his new cellmate which prompted a smile. "Hi, I'm Bob. " Bob extended his hand to Tyler as if they were in a business meeting.

Tyler was a bit taken back. It had been a while since anyone smiled at him, let alone extended a friendly handshake. Tyler noticed Bob was different from most guys who ended up here. Bob seemed polite. He didn't have that arrogant, tough-guy act so many prisoners seemed to carry around, and there wasn't even a hint of hatred or indignation. He seemed to be buoyed by some sort of optimism that was downright out of place.

It wasn't long before he figured out what was going on. The first morning, before the light crossed the cold cement floor, he woke and noticed Bob kneeling by the side of his bed. It looked like he was praying. Tyler rolled over in the darkness, turning his back on him. He didn't want to be a part of that nonsense.

Tyler hadn't always felt that way. He had taken his family to church on most Sundays and every holiday. He even prayed to God. That was before he lost his family. After that, he came to the conclusion God wasn't real. If he was, why would he have allowed such an awful thing to happen to his family? Why would God allow him to rot in this prison? Besides, what was the point of faith if the result of trying to live a good life was this? God was a myth the weak used to get through their lives.

Bob remained quiet during the first week, not forcing conversation. One morning when Tyler woke, rather than rolling over to turn his back, he watched Bob pray. Tyler thought he was being discrete, but evidently not.

"Good morning, Tyler." A warmth filled Bob's whisper.

Tyler remained quiet. *"Since when did a prisoner say good morning? This kid was clueless. There was nothing good about a morning in prison."*

Bob continued, whispering in the early morning. "I hope I didn't disturb you." He paused as if deciding if he would continue. "You seem curious about what I'm doing."

Tyler sighed. So much for avoiding a conversation. "No, not really. I know what you're doing, but if you think God is listening, I should tell you, God doesn't exist in this hell hole."

"Actually, He does."

Bob's confidence made Tyler uncomfortable. He hesitated before responding. He didn't want to be mean, but Bob was in for a rude awakening. "You believe what you want. I don't mean to shatter your hopes, but you'll see in time. God doesn't rescue people from here."

"You might be right Tyler, but he can USE people from here."

Tyler rolled over and turned his back on Bob. He didn't want to hear a sermon. This kid had no idea how this place would wear him down, and how his idealistic thoughts of God would erode away. He hadn't been through his first holiday alone. He hadn't spent night after night, thinking of what should have been. He hadn't kissed his wife one final time. He'd yet to endure the jeers of the inmates for days on end nor their abuse, especially if he continued to claim his innocence. No one believes in innocence in here; not when it comes to child abusers. Poor kid. His punishment was just beginning. If believing an almighty God was going to help him get through, more power to him.

31

ASHLEY

Ashley felt a chill of excitement as she entered the courthouse. Months of hard stuff filled her calendar, but today she would be celebrating Heather and Dave's adoption of fifteen-month-old Thad. They had been his foster parents since birth.

Although reunification with his biological mother Joann had been the goal, she failed to complete her parenting and treatment plans. Ashley had confronted her. "You've had a treatment plan for a year now and you continue to have dirty UA's."

"I want to stop, but I can't."

"Joann, we want to help you, but you have to want to be helped. You have to work the plan."

"I'm trying."

"Are you? You haven't made it to any visits with Thad for the last five months."

"I've had to work, and my boyfriend wouldn't give me a ride."

"Those are excuses and you know it. Thad needs a permanent home."

"I know." Tears filled her eyes as she rubbed the back of her neck. "I don't know what to do."

"I think it's time we consider other options. We are at a point of recommending the courts sever your parental rights so Thad can be adopted."

A tear rolled down Joann's cheek as she stared at her lap.

"Joann, talk to me. What are you thinking?"

Joann lifted her head. "I love him." She paused and a sob escaped as she added, "But I can't take care of him. It sounds like his foster family is good to him."

"Yes, they love him very much. He's growing and developing as a healthy child should."

"That's good. I was afraid I might have hurt him during my pregnancy."

"You did Joann. He has signs of fetal alcohol syndrome, and we don't know what the long-term effects of your meth use might be, but he is in a home where he is loved. They will make sure he gets the help he needs.

Both women were quiet for a moment. "Joann, you could relinquish your parental rights rather than having a judge do it."

Joann nodded her head. "Yes, that would probably be best." Another tear fell, leaving a dark stain on her jeans. "I hope he won't hate me."

Ashley reached to squeeze her hand. "Choosing what is best for your son is the most selfless, loving thing you can do for him."

She nodded again. "I've been thinking about it. I don't want to lose him, but I can't seem to do what's right."

"This is a big decision. The most important thing is what's best for Thad."

Joann inhaled and a shuttered breath came out. "I want him to have a family. I can't give him anything. I'll sign the papers."

Ashley had already prepared the documents. She knew they would be at this crossroads soon. Joann's hand shook as she signed the document. She sat back in her chair, swiping at her tears with the sleeves of her shirt. Ashley put her arm around her shoulders and gave her a hug. "You made a brave and selfless decision."

"Thank you for making sure my baby has a good home." With that, Joann stood and rushed from the room. Ashley felt a mix of sadness, knowing Joann was hurting, but joy for Heather and Dave who would soon be celebrating.

Ashley proceeded to file the papers and called Heather. "I have news. You might want to sit down. Thad's mom has relinquished her parental rights. You can adopt him."

"Are you serious? I can't believe it."

"It's true."

Heather's giggle intertwined with a sob. "I need to call Dave. Oh, Ashley, thank you so much. I'm going to be a mother."

That was three months ago. Now they were here, celebrating Thad's adoption. When she entered the judge's chambers, Heather rushed to hug her. Dave followed, carrying darling little Thad, dressed in a striped dress shirt, bow tie, and dress pants, sucking on a pacifier. "Thank you so much for coming." Heather's face beamed with joy.

"I wouldn't miss this for the world."

The courtroom generally felt stifling, but today felt different. A sense of joy filled the air. The balloons someone brought added to that feeling. Soon Judge Thomas summoned Heather and Dave.

Ashley stepped back, blending into the crowd of happy extended family members who ranged from little cousins to aunts, uncles, and grandparents. Looking around, she couldn't keep from smiling. What a gift this boy would receive today, this group of people would become his forever family. If only he understood the significance of this occasion.

The judge interrupted her thoughts, "I understand we are here for the adoption of little Thad." The smile on his face indicated he enjoyed this celebration as well.

Dave spoke up, "Yes."

"What a beautiful occasion to celebrate. Thank you for the privilege of being part of this." He gave a tender nod in Dave and Heather's direction. He continued, "Let me get through a few legal issues." He verified the names and birthdates of both Heather and Dave as well as Thad's. Then he began.

He looked at Dave and Heather. "Do you intend to raise Thad as your own son, as if he were your biological child?"

"Yes." They responded simultaneously.

"Are you willing to accept responsibility for raising this child?"

"Yes." Heather's eyes misted over as she raised her hand to wipe away a tear.

"Do you intend to provide for his needs physically, emotionally, and spiritually?"

"Yes."

The judge turned toward the extended family. "Are you, as Thad's extended family, willing to love and care for Thad as if he were your biological relative?"

All members of the family nodded in agreement. Sweet yesses echoed in the room.

"I hereby declare Thad David Jones is a member of the Jones family forever. Congratulations."

Thad wiggled in Dave's arms the entire ceremony so Dave set him on the floor. Thad took off like a bullet as he explored the courtroom from his perspective. Heather, hot on his trail, kept him from touching things he shouldn't.

Ashley's heart felt full as she observed the extended family swarm around Heather, Dave, and Thad. This is what every little boy deserved. This is what made her job so rewarding.

She knew she should go and leave the family to this moment, but she needed to savor this experience. It had been a hard season of life. This reenergized her. As she leaned her head against the wall, she closed her eyes and listened as the family offered congratulations. Laughter filled the air. Thad babbled, "Mama." She wished she could bottle up the joy in this room and save it for when she had those hard days.

She felt someone press her arm. Opening her eyes, she saw Heather. "I didn't want you to leave before I could say thank you. I don't know how we would have gotten through this without you."

Ashley smiled and gave Heather a gentle hug. "I'm so happy for you and your family, for Thad. Congratulations."

Heather put her hand on Ashley's arm. "You have been so kind. You made me feel like Thad's mom, even though I wasn't."

You are, Heather. You're his mother in every sense."

Heather swallowed and looked away, seeming to gather herself. "Thank you for saying that. At times I didn't feel like it."

"What do you mean?"

"I remember once when Thad was sick, I didn't want to do his immunizations. I wanted to wait until he felt better, but the doctor ignored my concerns." She blinked and took a breath. "I was just the foster mom."

Ashley never heard this perspective. She gave Heather another hug.

Heather had more to say. "When I went to visit friends, I felt like my role as his mom was discredited. They didn't understand I loved Thad as much as they loved their children. My nights were just as short as other new moms and yet, very few people even asked if I was getting any sleep. It was as if I wasn't a real mom." She paused and looked at the floor. Then she looked at Ashley again. "No one offered to host a baby shower nor acknowledged a baby joined our family, but you always treated me like I was important to Thad. I don't know if you can understand how much that meant to me."

Ashley hadn't felt like she'd done anything special. She had just done her job, but Heather's words moved her. "I'm so happy for you Heather. I'm so glad Thad has a family."

Heather smiled. "Thank you again Ashley. You made us a family."

"No, that was God." She was careful about speaking of her faith, but today it felt like the most appropriate thing to say.

"That may be true Ashley. You did a very good job of working as God's assistant. We will never forget you."

32

TYLER

Tyler never wanted to know much about his cell mates. What was the point? It wasn't like he would be having a neighborhood barbeque with these guys once they got out. In fact, the less he knew about them, the better. Besides, most of them deserved to be here. They were guilty.

It did make for a lonely existence. He had adjusted though. There were those in his "group" who watched out for each other on the grounds and at meal times, but they didn't share details of their lives. At least not until Bob arrived.

In the months they had been cell mates, Bob had grown on him. Bob continued to believe he would get his day in court. "I'm telling you Tyler, my attorney is smart and he's working hard to get the truth out. I'm going to go home to my family."

"I hope you're right." Tyler had to give him credit for keeping his optimistic spirit.

"I am. You wait and see."

"You deserve it man." Tyler shifted from one foot to the other.

Bob was on a roll. He wasn't letting up. "You've got to meet my attorney. I think he could help you too."

How many times had Bob tried to line him up with his attorney? He should have been a matchmaker with his tenacity. Tyler shook his head. "I don't know. It's been a long time. There's not much to salvage anymore."

"He can't give you your twenty-five years back, but you deserve to have your honor cleared. Maybe he could even help you reconnect with your family."

Tyler remained quiet. Why let a spark of hope begin? He'd spent a considerable amount of time through the years squelching hope. The more Bob talked, the more he wondered. Was it possible? He didn't let on to Bob. If Bob thought he gave it a moment's thought, he'd never let it drop.

"My family has moved on. I can't imagine they would want me to be part of their lives anymore." His heart hurt even saying the words. He'd love to see his kids or at least know they were okay. He'd love to start over with Sarah, but she had a new life. The divorce papers made that clear. Yet, even though she was no longer his wife, a day never passed when he didn't think of her. She was the one nice thought that allowed him to consider his life hadn't been a total waste, even if this is how it turned out. It would have been nice to grow old with her.

Bob interrupted his thoughts. "Tyler, you might be surprised. Wouldn't you at least like to know what happened to your family? Maybe get to know them? What would be the harm in checking into it? You have two months before you'll be released, right? What then? Come on man. Think about it!"

Tyler shook his head. No matter how persuasive Bob tried to be, the answer never changed. "No, it wouldn't be fair to them. I'm not the same person I was back then."

"I don't buy that. You're not like the rest of these guys. You might think you've changed, but there is still a very good, kind person under that shell. Once you get out of here, you should spend some time letting that person grow again."

Tyler shook his head. What did this kid know? Sure, they both had children taken by CPS. They both ended up here and after hearing Bob's story, Tyler knew Bob was also innocent, but that ended their similarities. Tyler didn't share Bob's optimistic spirit or faith, nor did he want to. When he returned to the outside world in a few months, he'd try to find a job, a cheap place to live, and forget his past.

Bob kept at it. In the confines of their cell, it wasn't like Tyler could get away. Plus, Bob's confidence was refreshing. Tyler could almost feel himself coming to life. In the quiet of the night, he began to ponder if there could be more to his life.

33

ASHLEY

When RT and Ashley met over dinner several weeks later, he greeted her, but then got quiet. He looked over the menu, but kept staring at the same page. She glanced at him several times, but he never looked up.

The waitress came to take their order. "Have you decided?"

"Uh. No. Can we get a few more minutes?" He gazed out the window and then back to the menu.

"You seem like you are miles away."

"Oh, I'm so sorry. Yes, I have a lot on my mind. I probably shouldn't have come tonight. I might bore you."

"Are you kidding? I love to hear what you're doing. I've never worked on the other side of crime." She bit her lip. She'd done it again, creating a conflict between their work rather than looking for common ground.

He remained stoic. "I took a case that has gotten under my skin. I can't discuss it. Your department is involved."

She knew she better keep her mouth shut. She couldn't trust herself to refrain from some sarcastic remark, especially if he defended child abusers. Oh man, this was the wrong guy to get involved with. The silence went too long. "So why did you take on a child abuser?"

"Because he's innocent."

"How can you be so certain?" Her question came out with more sarcasm than she intended.

"What? Just because a guy is accused of child abuse, that makes him guilty?"

The intensity of his question surprised her. "No, I didn't say that, but I've seen so much abuse and neglect. Maybe I'm a bit biased."

"So am I." His words were firm and direct. "My parents were accused of neglect. That's why we were taken away, but they never hurt us. They loved us. Someone should have helped them, defended them, but no one did."

So, that's where he got his passion for being a defense attorney. Didn't he know all children think their parents are innocent, even if they get slapped around and mistreated? No matter how badly they are treated, they believe their parents love them. That's not love! She didn't dare say so. Clearly, he was not going to be convinced otherwise.

"I've got to help this man. If someone would have helped my parents, my life would have been so much different. I don't know if you've ever noticed, but when you are dealing with criminal law, the accused are considered innocent until proven guilty. In family law, if someone is accused of child abuse or neglect, they are guilty. Period! Everyone treats them as if they're guilty. This guy is innocent and I'm going to prove it."

"You seem so sure." She tried not to betray her disbelief. She didn't want to start an argument. She wanted to understand.

"I've heard his story. I believe him. Besides, sometimes you just know. Doesn't that happen in your line of work too?"

Ashley thought of the many cases where she'd taken children from horrible situations. She knew those children had been abused or neglected. She had proof. She'd seen the homes and the parents who cared so little for their children. What made RT so sure?

He seemed to know her thoughts as he eyed her with a suspicious look. "You need to hear my client's story. His trial starts in a couple weeks. You've been giving me a hard time about seeing me defend the innocent. Here's your chance." The lines in his face seemed deeper than usual. His eyes were piercing. Depending on how this case went, this could be a deal breaker for their relationship. Then again, perhaps she needed to listen with a different perspective and keep an open mind. She was curious.

"I just might do that." Her words were measured.

"Good, because you might find your way of thinking will be challenged a bit. I have a strong feeling even you will have to admit my client is innocent." He seemed determined to make his point. "I mean no disrespect for what you do Ashley. I know most CPS caseworkers are like you, concerned about children and their safety, but there are caseworkers who have wrong motives."

She felt the hair on the back of her neck go up as she raised her eyebrows. What was he accusing them of?

He continued. "Again, I mean no disrespect. Just as there are good cops and bad cops, good lawyers and bad lawyers, there are good caseworkers and bad ones. Unfortunately, in my time in the system, I saw plenty of bad ones. I hesitated to get into this before. I didn't want to scare you off. I really like you, Ashley. Like I mentioned before, when I found out what you did for a living, it set me back. I wasn't sure I could date a woman who worked for CPS because of my own negative experiences."

So, he considered them dating now? She remained quiet and RT continued. She wanted to hear him out even though this conversation had become uncomfortable.

"I've spent a lot of time through the years trying to figure out how my life got so derailed. I could never understand why my parents were treated so poorly. Why my voice as a child was never considered. I had no rights. My words were ignored. Going into law allowed me to access legal matters. I've had the chance to look into cases and get insights into foster care. To be honest, the system is broken."

She felt the need to defend herself. "I would agree. There are too many cases to handle and it's impossible to keep up. There is too much paperwork that takes time away from helping children. There isn't enough money to hire enough qualified people and addictions are rampant, causing families to fall apart, placing a burden on an already strained system."

"That is all true Ashley, but there's more to it than that."

"Like what?"

"Like corruption and greed."

Ashley bit her lip again. That comment didn't even deserve a response. So, she waited, trying to cool the fire that stirred in her soul.

He took a breath and blew it out slowly. "I'm sorry if I hit a nerve, but it's true."

"Perhaps you should explain." A coolness filled her voice.

"Do you think in all cases, a child is better off once they've been removed from their homes?"

She wanted to keep her emotions in check. "In the cases I've worked, the children are only removed when they aren't safe so, yes."

"In those cases, do the children suffer any trauma once they've been removed?"

"Of course. They have already suffered trauma from what happened in their home. And yes, they suffer more trauma once they're removed. It's hard on kids to be separated from their home and family, even if it's unsafe. Children often see their own abusive home as better than a safe foster home, at least initially. We have to do what is in their best interest."

"I'm not going to debate that with you right now, but let me ask you, how much more traumatic do you think it is for a child when they are removed from a home where they have NOT been abused or neglected?"

"I guess I don't understand. A child wouldn't be removed unless they were abused or neglected."

"Not true. Sometimes children get removed because CPS doesn't agree with a family's personal decisions, like vaccinations or medical choices made for a child. Most children are removed from their homes because of neglect, which can be very subjective. Children have been removed after a caseworker disagreed with a midwife doing a home delivery. CPS has stepped in when children were allowed to walk home from a park, or when an accident occurred, or even for homeschooling. I've even heard of cases where children were taken after a sibling died of Sudden Infant Death."

"I've never seen that."

"No, I suspect you haven't. However, do you think it's possible, in a city this size, there are caseworkers who are taking children away because of their own biases, just as cops might arrest a black kid due to their own biases?"

"I can't imagine..."

"Can't imagine or not possible?"

"I guess anything is possible." She tripped over the last word with a stutter. "Why would a CPS worker take a child under those circumstances, especially when we have so many cases already?"

"In some cases, the caseworkers lack the experience or training to make the right decision. With high turnover, you have less experienced staff. They make mistakes. In other cases, greed and corruption exist."

"That's preposterous." That's the second time he'd alluded to that and she found it downright offensive. She could feel her face flush as she crossed her arms over her body.

"Ashley, what's really preposterous is because there are so many children flooding the system for the wrong reasons, the children that really need the help aren't getting it."

Ashley clenched her hands in her lap. "I don't think you're being fair, RT. While I agree we are overloaded, we work hard to rescue only children who are abused and neglected."

"I don't doubt that, Ashley. I'm not trying to start a fight. It's just there's a lot of stuff going on that isn't right. The safety of children isn't always the first consideration. Let's face it. If money is involved, and there is big money in foster care, then there is room for corruption. It's possible you aren't aware of such cases because they're being diverted to other caseworkers who are willing to play the game."

"You're saying this is a game?"

"No, not at all. In my opinion, it's more like a crime. Think about it. There are layers of professionals who benefit from children in foster care. Caseworkers, their supervisors, court-appointed attorneys for the children, state-approved counselors and evaluators, state-approved doctors, court clerks, prosecutors, judges, district attorneys; the list goes on and on. Now suppose instead of more children in foster care, there are fewer. How many people would lose part of their income or maybe even their job? Ashley, foster care and adopting out children has become big business."

Ashley glared at RT.

He put his hands in the air, looking as if he were surrendering. "Hey, don't take my word for it. Check it out for yourself. Laws put into place to reduce the number of children in foster care has had the opposite effect. Just Google CAPTA. I don't have to tell you. Look at how the number of children in foster care has exploded. As a result, funding has increased."

Her lips hurt from pinching them together. She shook her head back and forth as if to deny what he implied. Yet, in the back of her mind, a seed of doubt had been planted. What if he was right? What if greed drove the increase in the number of children in foster care? It seemed unthinkable. "Our agency is devoted to doing what is in the best interest of the child, PERIOD."

"Really? Because a child's best interest is not always happening for foster kids. As you mentioned before, any child removed from their home will experience trauma. Research shows those children will experience developmental delays. Some experience more abuse or even death while in their foster families."

Her mind snapped back to the child James had been overseeing, the one who died in the meth house. As she thought of that little boy, she felt her own defensiveness melting. Maybe RT was onto something.

He continued driving home his point. "Often children struggle with mental illness or become addicts as a result of their experience in foster care. Many suffer from PTSD. Others lose all contact with their families, including their siblings. If they remain in the system for an extended period and aren't adopted, they age out with no family at all. For those kids, the outcomes aren't great. Few go to college, let alone graduate. Many of them populate the homeless shelters and prisons. Over half of children rescued from sex trafficking have been foster kids. As a society, we are failing children in foster care."

"So, what's the solution?"

"There needs to be a return to what is in the best interests of the children. In cases where the family might need support to get back on their feet, we need to help the family stay together. It would be a lot better to help a single mom repair her car so she can work, rather than to take her kids because she can't feed them without a job and a car to get her there."

Ashley nodded in agreement.

"And in cases where the parents are using drugs or alcohol, if possible, help them get sober while keeping the family together, as long as the children are safe. That way everyone gets help as a family unit. As you know, trying to reunite a family once the children have experienced trauma from separation is hard to do, especially if the separation goes on for a long time. By helping the family as a whole, there is a chance to break the cycle rather than perpetuating it."

"So, would these solutions have helped your family?"

RT looked down at the table. He remained quiet for a moment. When he looked up, he answered with a slow sad whisper. "No, it wouldn't have."

"Why not?"

"Because my parents didn't abuse or neglect us. They weren't addicts. My parents simply needed a good lawyer."

"Therefore, you became a lawyer."

He nodded. Quiet hesitation froze in the air.

Ashley hated to ask the next question and yet, she had to. "So how do you know so much about what happened to your parents?"

"I've looked into the case, and I remember..." His voice cracked.

She felt like she pushed him too far. She wished she could take her question back, but there was nowhere to go but forward. "Why were you put in foster care?"

He rubbed his hand over his chin and looked down again. Then his gaze penetrated her with a sadness she had seen only in the children she'd rescued. "Someday I'll tell you, but it is still very painful to talk about. Bottom line; CPS used a legal loophole to destroy my family. You're probably familiar with the phrase: 'at the discretion of the department'."

She nodded. She'd used department discretion herself when she felt a child was in imminent danger. She'd never thought of it the way RT presented it, as a way to destroy a family.

He interrupted her thoughts. "However, if I couldn't live with my parents, given a choice, I'd have preferred to live with an uncle, or maybe even a children's home."

"Like an orphanage?" She gasped.

"Sort of, but not like the Annie type orphanages with cruel house mothers." He smiled.

She couldn't help but smile. "So, tell me about this."

"The successful ones are often run by private organizations. Under the supervision of house parents, children live together and become a new family unit. It gives kids a permanent home rather than bouncing them around like I was."

She nodded, thinking of little Michael who might never find another adoptive family after his first adoption failed.

RT continued to talk. "It would have been a good fit for me since I didn't want to be adopted. Other kids are too old, have a disability, have some sort of history that keeps them from getting adopted. A children's home, if it's done right, can give kids a sense of belonging to a family again."

"Wow, RT. You're really passionate about this."

"That's the result of a foster kid turned attorney." A wry smile began to creep across his face.

She was relieved to see his demeanor lighten. She knew her motivation for being a caseworker, but could he be right? Could there be corruption driving foster care beyond the best interests of children? Were there better ways to help families and their children that didn't create more trauma? She knew she needed some time to process everything, but not tonight. She had a killer headache. She needed to go home, take an aspirin, and get to bed.

"RT, I don't think I can adequately express how sorry I am for what you went through."

He blinked a few times.

"I appreciate what you've shared tonight. However, I need to call it a night. It's been a very long day."

"You're right. It has been a long day. I hope I didn't bore you." His smile faded.

"No, not at all. I enjoyed our visit very much, and you've given me a lot to think about. So, thank you."

He reached up to rub the back of his neck as his gaze went to the table top. He looked beaten, having exposed such a vulnerable part of his life.

She wanted to pull him into her arms and hold him. Her heart skipped a beat at the thought of him being that close. She reached over to touch his arm. "Hey RT, I really mean that. This has been very enlightening."

He nodded.

She rose to stand and as she did, he stood to pull out her chair. Her heart hammered as they stood together. She put her arm around his waist and gave him a hug.

He pulled her closer, returned the hug, and placed a kiss on her forehead. "Thanks for the wonderful visit." Emotion thickened his voice. He cleared his throat. "I'd love to see you at my court case."

"I'll do my best. Really, I'll try." She felt such an urge to kiss him, but stepped away. She couldn't let this go any further, at least not yet. They had too many differences to work through. If he defended child abusers, it was only a matter of time before they would be sitting on opposite sides of the same case. "Again, thank you. I'll see you soon RT."

"I hope so." His eyes were dark and intense as he nodded in agreement.

As Ashley drove to her apartment, their conversation lingered. His childhood, the idea of helping families before their children were removed, the children's home, helping children to feel like they belong in a family. What stuck in her mind most was his suggestion children were being removed unnecessarily from good homes for reasons beyond sinister. Was that really possible? Could his parents have been innocent?

She thought of her own family. She had been so blessed. Then a torturous thought hit her. What if, like RT's family, her own biological family had been victimized and misunderstood? What if she had been removed and placed up for adoption for reasons other than abuse or neglect? Her headache seemed to magnify at the thought. One thing was certain, she needed to find out.

34

ASHLEY

When Ashley woke the next morning, her headache was gone. She needed to be on her game with her current workload.

When she arrived at work, she noticed several of her coworkers whispering in the hall. Although she enjoyed most of her coworkers, these two in particular seemed to have grown calloused to the job. As she made her way past them, they paused their whispering. Fine with her. She didn't want to know what they were talking about, likely just gossip anyway.

As soon as she stepped beyond them, one of them spoke loud enough for her to hear. "I don't care if he's innocent. I know a family that would love that baby, and Robin indicated she'd like me to make the adoption happen."

She was stunned. An innocent father? It took everything in her to not turn on her heels and go back to question the women, but she proceeded down the hall to her office. The comment lingered. She thought of her conversation with RT. Could he be right about wrongful accusations? Could there be wrong motives in some of the cases? And could the father they referred to, be the client RT represented?

She flipped on her light and sat at her desk. The Acer children's file caught her eye. She had yet to find a foster home where they could be together. It bothered her that they might grow up without each other. Now that she thought about it, there were a number of things that bothered her lately. The conversation she'd overheard in the hall. The staff meeting last week when her supervisor Robin congratulated several of her co-workers for bringing in more children than the previous week. What was that about?

Ashley sighed. She needed to focus. Turning her attention to her desktop calendar, she noticed a yellow sticky note: Nichole's file. It must still be on Robin's desk waiting for her signature. She'd better check on it.

As Ashley made her way down the hall, she thought of how much progress Nichole had made. After passing out drunk, at the Walmart parking lot with her children in her car, she sobered up and made significant steps in her recovery. Ashley recommended moving toward reunification.

Robin's door was open so Ashley tapped and poked her head in. She smiled. "Good morning. I'm just following up on the report for Nichole and her children."

Robin looked up, but didn't return Ashley's smile. "Yes, I've been meaning to talk to you about this. I've looked this over. I don't agree with your assessment. Nichole isn't ready for reunification."

Ashley felt her face flush. She stepped into the office and stood up straight. "Is there a reason you don't think she's ready?"

"Yes, two failed drug tests indicate she's still using. I'd like you to change the recommendation. Let's face it. We need to be prepared to terminate parental rights and allow the children to be adopted."

"Those failed tests can be explained. She attended a family funeral out-of-town and failed to notify the clinic she'd be gone. The other was the day she started her new job. She was so excited about the job; she forgot about the test. That's still twenty-eight clean tests."

"Those are not legitimate excuses. She needed thirty clean UA's." Robin's tone was aggressive.

Ashley knew she'd better tread lightly, but she had to advocate for Nichole. She had been working so hard. Ashley took a breath to keep her voice in check. "Robin, I understand your concerns, but this family is making progress. Nichole arrived on time for every

147

visit and her children are always happy to see her. She's working her program. I would hate to keep their family apart any longer because we both know the longer the parent goes without their children, the more likely they will give up."

"Healthy parents don't need a reason to be good parents."

"I realize that, but Nichole is on the right track to being a healthy, responsible parent. Starting the reunification process will help Nichole complete her program, to stay clean. Even more important, I believe it's best for the children. They need to be with their mom."

A muscle tightened in Robin's jaw. She gave Ashley an icy stare. Ashley realized her comments hadn't been appreciated and might even be considered insubordination. Robin pulled Nichole's file from her stack, opened it and spent a few minutes looking through the pages. The silence grew uncomfortable.

Ashley bit her lip. She had said too much and yet, had it made any difference?

Robin looked up from the file. Her words came out in a spat. "Okay, we'll delay termination, but reunification needs to be delayed as well. At least until there are ten more clean UA's."

"Okay. Thank you." She exhaled a deep breath. Not what she'd hoped for, but better than what Robin suggested. Termination of Nichole's parental rights? When Nichole had been working so hard! That seemed unfair.

When she left Robin's office, a horrible, gnawing feeling filled her stomach. Her face felt hot. A bead of sweat trickled down her back. Was this what it was going to be like working for Robin? She couldn't imagine having to fight her own supervisor to help deserving families be reunited. Granted, there were numerous families who didn't deserve more chances. The horrific abuse or neglect they perpetrated on their children was deplorable and inexcusable, but Nichole was different. She deserved another chance.

35
RT

It had been a long hard day. RT ran into a number of obstacles with his recent case. As he left the office, exhaustion accompanied him. He looked up and noticed a dark cloud in the distance. If he hurried, he could grab dinner before it started to rain. He stopped at the neighborhood market and picked up a deli sandwich and salad. As an afterthought, he grabbed a six pack of beer.

At his apartment, he flipped on the lights. The starkness of his studio apartment caused him to let out a sigh. He hadn't lived here long as evidenced by the lack of pictures on the wall. It's not as if he had any family pictures to hang anyway. Tonight, it felt lonely.

He dropped his jacket on a chair, loosened his tie, kicked his dress shoes to the closet, and changed into more comfortable sweat clothes. Grabbing the remote, he turned on the TV. The local news just started. The first story featured a child who had been abducted. Just what he didn't want to hear about. He switched the channel and popped open a beer.

He dropped into his favorite chair and let out a sigh. He needed to get some work done tonight, but for now, it felt good to relax. Taking a swig, he tasted the cool brew. A tingly sensation filled his throat as it went down. The familiar taste reminded him...

He shouldn't have picked up these beers. He'd worked too hard to get past that part of his life. He started drinking alcohol at twelve years of age. Back then, it helped to numb his pain, a perfect thing to hide in a bottle. By the age of thirteen, he was drinking every night. On occasion he threw in some drugs. Nothing hard core, just enough to deaden his senses and forget the past.

A couple times he came close to getting caught with alcohol, but somehow managed to skate by unnoticed. That really shouldn't have surprised him. No one noticed him, not his foster parents, the kids in the group home, or the CPS caseworkers. He might as well have been invisible.

He managed to stay in school where he could get a hot meal at lunchtime and keep the truancy officer off his back. When he was sixteen, a buddy of his died over a drug deal. He could see the writing on the wall. If he didn't clean up his act, he was headed for the same outcome. He lay low for a while and then joined the military, but that didn't help him with his alcohol issues. In fact, it only made it worse, since drinking helped him feel like a part of the brotherhood.

Then a year into the military, a wild party followed by a bar fight landed him in the brig. His commanding officer gave him a work out the next day that left him retching. That was enough. He knew he'd let alcohol take control of his life. He needed to make some changes. He needed help. That's when he started talking to the military counselor, joined a support group to start facing his demons, and began to unpack his childhood.

His childhood; it had been a long time since he'd given any thought to it. It eased into the edges of his mind tonight, perhaps due to his conversations with Ashley, or perhaps because of his new client. Regardless, tonight the memories were back, taunting him.

He remembered that first night away from his parents. He was only seven. His little sister Leanna had cried, and he'd tried to comfort her. He was so scared, but he had to be strong for her. He was the big brother which made him in charge, at least until they could go home.

It felt as if weeks passed before they saw his mom. A lady caseworker took them to a big building where his mom waited. He wondered why they didn't go home. He remembered the room where they met. The orange paint peeled off the wall and the room smelled odd, like a baby's room when diapers are left there. He remembered the ominous mirror, like he'd seen in the movies. He knew someone had to be on the other side watching them.

When he saw his mom, her face was streaked with tears she'd tried to cover with makeup. She hugged him until he thought he would smother.

He remembered the first question he'd asked her. "Where's Daddy?"

Her response seemed scripted. "There has been a terrible mistake. Daddy can't come right now, but he sends his love." She tried to talk without crying which made her voice sound muffled.

"Why did the police come and put handcuffs on him?"

"Oh, son. I wish you hadn't seen that." Her eyes were sad.

"Why did daddy have to go to jail?" He remembered how confused he felt. No one would tell him what was going on. It scared him.

She started to cry and shook as she spoke. "They think he…that he..." She couldn't even finish the sentence, but he knew how it ended. They thought his daddy hurt Noah and made him die.

Thinking of it made him shiver, just like it did as a little boy. From his seven-year-old perspective, if anyone was to blame, it was him. That day at the pool, Daddy had been helping Leanna on the slide and asked him to keep an eye on Noah. Ryan had encouraged little Noah to jump off the side of the pool. He should have caught Noah before his head went under. If that's why Noah died, then he was the one who killed him. He dared not tell anyone though. If he did, he might go to jail too.

Every week his mom came to visit him, but never Daddy. Leanna stopped coming too. He feared something happened to her. Maybe she'd died or been put in jail too. He wondered if the same thing would happen to him, but he didn't dare ask, so he continued to keep his secret.

With each visit, he was happy to see his mom, but missed his dad. He missed Leanna and Noah too. Mom brought gifts and games and while they played, she would run her cool fingers through his hair and rub his back with her fingertips. Often, he'd hear quiet sobs as she tried to hide her tears. Something very bad was going on and he wished she would tell him.

At the end of the visits, the lady caseworker would open the door and tell him to say goodbye to his mom. His mom would pull him into another tight hug and whisper, "I love you son. I'll be back soon. I promise. And soon we'll go home together."

The caseworker took his hand and led him down the hall. He remembered her tugging at him, trying to make him walk faster. At the last possible moment, he looked back over his shoulder to see his mom. She was still there, waving and blowing kisses. Although smiling, he could see she was trying not to cry.

This went on for a long time, but one week the caseworker didn't come to take him to see his mom. Soon after he moved to a home and was told he would have a new family. He figured his parents discovered the truth about Noah. They must be mad at him for not being honest, and disappointed he allowed Dad to take the blame for Noah's death. They must have decided to give him away. He didn't really blame them. He didn't deserve to be their son anymore.

With the truth out, his shame and guilt multiplied and grew into anger. He was angry at his parents for breaking their promise to come and get him, and at the caseworker who told him he would get a nice new home when all he wanted was his own home. The anger at himself boiled hot. If he'd caught Noah, none of this would have happened. If anyone deserved his anger, it was him for allowing Noah to get hurt. He deserved all the anger and pain he felt because he had allowed this to happen.

So, when the Ellington's asked him if it would be okay if they adopted him, he agreed. They seemed nice. After living in that last group home, with those mean boys who urinated on him while he slept, a new home might be okay. Besides, it had been a long time since he'd seen his mom. It didn't look as though he had a family anymore.

He settled into his new school and didn't tell anyone about his past. His secrets were his sentence; losing his family was his prison.

After he lived with his new parents for a while, they pulled him aside and told him his adoption had been approved. He thought he'd already been adopted. The next morning, they instructed him to dress up in new clothes, so he did. Hand-in-hand they went into a big building and stood before a judge. The judge looked like a giant sitting behind the tall desk. It scared him.

The judge asked him, "Do you want to be adopted by Mr. and Mrs. Ellington?" He didn't know what to say. He didn't want to disappoint these nice people or make the judge mad. He remembered biting his lower lip between his teeth so he wouldn't cry. When the judge asked again, he answered, "Yes." It seemed the only way to escape the truth of his crime.

After the judge talked some more, he told Ryan his last name was now Ellington. His new parents gave him hugs and told him how happy they were. They stood in a row to take pictures. He knew he had to smile big, so he did, but deep down, he wanted to cry. It felt like his life was crumbling apart. This wasn't his family, but now that he agreed to be adopted, he'd never get his own family back. He killed his brother and allowed his dad to go to jail. He was someone else's son. That made him a traitor. What kind of a son traded his own family for another?

*　　*　　*　　*　　*

RT woke to a headache the size of Texas. He must have fallen asleep on the couch. His neck felt stiff as a board so he rolled his head around, hoping to loosen it up. As he did, he noticed six empty beer bottles on the coffee table. He groaned as regret hit him like a punch to the stomach. What a fool to have drunk all those beers. How careless to allow old habits to ease into his life. A beer with Ashley, a drink with his buddies after a court case, and now a whole six pack. He knew he was playing with fire.

Running his hands through his hair, he thought of the previous night's journey down memory lane. It had taken years for him to come to terms with the fact that Noah's death wasn't his fault. It wasn't anyone's fault; just a tragic accident. Even so, he had a hard time letting go of the tragedy of that day, especially knowing his dad went to jail as an innocent man. How could a fair judicial system have allowed that?

Thoughts of Ashley popped into his mind. He remembered her sympathetic, yet unconvinced look when he shared his dad's innocence. She didn't get it. If anyone knew that to be true, it was he. Yet, the truth never mattered, even now when he told others about it. That injustice had driven him as he worked toward his law degree. Innocent men didn't deserve to rot in prison. Innocent men didn't deserve to lose their families. If he had his way, it was going to happen a lot less. Maybe it would make up for losing his own family.

A lump found its way to his throat. His family! What happened to them? Why did he continue to torment himself with a past he could no longer recapture? He attempted to search for them a few times, but all he learned was his dad remained in prison, and when it came down to it, he wasn't sure what he'd even say to them.

He stumbled to the shower to clear his head. Turning on the faucet, warm water poured over his face. He tried to focus on the tasks of the day ahead. He had a meeting with his client Bob to go over his case. He believed in Bob's innocence as much as he believed in his own father's. Bob was exactly the kind of person he wanted to defend. Perhaps he could save this man from injustice.

Continuing to think about his day, he regretted he wasn't as prepared as he would like since he'd fallen asleep on the couch. He'd need to work double time to get ready, and before the day ended, he'd better find his way to an AA meeting.

36

ASHLEY

As Ashley pulled into the parking lot of her office, it startled her to see people lined up on the sidewalk, carrying signs. It looked like they were protesting. They weren't loud or obnoxious, just milling around talking to each other.

She stepped out of her car, only letting one foot land on the pavement before looking around, checking for danger. Perhaps she should get back in and drive away. One of the protestors caught her eye. She hesitated. The woman didn't seem threatening. In fact, she seemed vulnerable. The sadness in her eyes was deep and distressing. Since their eyes met, Ashley smiled, but the woman didn't return the smile, only blinking away tears as she continued her sad stare.

Ashley noticed the signs they were carrying. "CPS kidnapped my child." "Cash for Kids." "CPS abuses more children than abusers." And another: "False allegations are Abuse". Some of the protestors even wore masks as if they were afraid to be recognized. She couldn't imagine why they were protesting.

With a clip to her step, she walked with a brisk pace toward the front door of the office, refusing to make eye contact with anyone else.

Inside, a group of her coworkers gathered, discussing the commotion outside. Ashley turned to the secretary, "What is that about?"

"Oh, just some radicals." She waved her hand in the air as she rolled her eyes.

"About what?"

"Who knows. We're darned if we do and darned if we don't around here. You know how it goes. If a child gets hurt in our care, it's our fault. If a child gets hurt when they're not in our care, it's also our fault."

She nodded her head. Yes, she knew they were under scrutiny to make sure the children were protected, but in her five years as a caseworker, she'd never seen protestors before. Who would take it to this point? She wondered if the little boy who died in the meth house had anything to do with it.

She made her way back to her office. The protesters were still on her mind. What could their signs mean? False allegations? Children kidnapped? CPS abuses children? What was going on? As she attempted to think it out, her conversation with RT resurfaced. He had said something similar. Again, she wondered. Could it be true? Could CPS be taking children from families they shouldn't? She shook her head. It just didn't make sense and yet, RT had alluded to this in their recent conversation.

She decided to put it out of her head. She had too much work to do to be distracted. She turned her attention to the files sitting on her desk. They all represented children in need, children who lived in horrific conditions. She had seen their circumstances herself. Picking up the first file, she tried to focus, but the image of the woman in the parking lot, her sad eyes, stuck in her mind. They radiated with grief. Was it possible the woman had been mistreated or wrongly accused? She fought the urge to flee to the sidewalk and ask more questions, but that would be inappropriate. Talking to the protestors could be considered treason, especially after recent changes in her department, namely Robin.

The demands of work soon forced her mind into the cases before her. The day passed in a blur with phone calls and appointments. She glanced at the clock above her door; 7:00 p.m. She let out a groan. No wonder her back felt so stiff. She hadn't moved from her desk in hours. Time to call it a day. She took a few moments to straighten the files that were strewn across her desk and lock up confidential information. Her eyes caught her sticky note. FOR THE CHILDREN. Did her agency always do what was right for the children? She let out a sigh, too tired to ponder it right now.

As she turned out her office light, she glanced down the hallway. It appeared everyone else had left. Most of her co-workers had families to make dinner for, or children to pick up from ball games or practices, but she didn't need for her to rush home to her empty apartment. Although she loved the solitude of her home, she enjoyed the energy and passion of her work more. She didn't mind being the last person out, the one who turned out the lights for the night.

When she pushed open the outside door, she realized it was now dark. The streetlight illuminated her car, but out of the corner of her eye, she noticed a torn sign in the outdoor garbage can. The protesters. She'd forgotten about them. She felt a nervous clutch of uneasiness. Were they still there? She glanced around again. Other than the sign, nothing else evidenced the morning's activities. She locked the office door and hurried to her car.

Once in her car, she locked the door and let out a sigh of relief. That's when she noticed a piece of paper under her windshield wiper. Again, she looked around, making sure there was no threat in the area. She opened her door and snatched the paper from her windshield.

Although curious, she felt nervous in the parking lot, therefore decided to look at the paper when she got home. At the first stoplight, curiosity got the best of her, so while her car idled, she glanced at the paper. On one side, she read, "Please help me." A chill ran down her spine. The stoplight turned green. She'd have to read the rest at home.

* * * * *

Back at her apartment, Ashley dropped her purse on the counter and kicked off her heels. Flipping the light on over her dining room table, she plopped into a chair with the note still clutched in her hand. She was dying to read it. With care, she opened the folded piece of paper:

"I need help I saw you today you seem like a nice lady I raised my granddaughter since she was born five years ago I am only family she knows her mom is my daughter she is on drugs the father don't want nothing to do with her he wanted to get abortion when she wouldn't he beat her so my daughter left him I'm not rich but I love my granddaughter and I took good care of her 4 months ago they give her to the father and she screamed when they took her she don't know her father he is bad and she must be scared I can't sleep or eat I can't afford lawyer I don't know what to do please help Janet Jones"

The broken writing made it hard to understand, but the desperate tone was obvious and shook her to the core. She read it again. She thought of the woman in the parking lot, the one with the haunting sadness. Could she have left the note? Based on the note, she might be poor or uneducated, but that wasn't a reason to take a child away from her. If the father was abusive, she couldn't imagine why he'd be allowed to have the little girl.

It couldn't be one of her cases since none of this was familiar to her. As such, she really couldn't do much about it. If it wasn't her case, she had no right to voice her opinion. The unspoken rule in the office: Keep your nose in your own cases and the office runs smoothly. Yet, this seemed unfair to the grandmother and not in the best interests of this child.

She set the note down and began making the salad she planned for dinner. She couldn't get the note or the sad faced woman out of her mind. There had to be something she could do for that grandmother. At the very least, she could look into it tomorrow, maybe ask around. Perhaps the caseworker dealing with this case would be willing to share some details.

After dinner, she turned on the television. She must have dozed off. The 10:00 news came on and she snapped awake. The reporter covered the morning protest. She listened with interest as several protestors shared their stories. Most participants identified themselves as grandparents. They all voiced concern for their grandchildren whom they lost contact with after being taken by CPS.

A tight knot formed in her throat. She thought of her own grandparents. She adored them. As an only child, her grandparents and extended family had been very important in her life. She couldn't imagine life without them. They, in many ways, had been more influential in her life than her parents. They spent many special times together while her parents traveled for anniversary weekends or couples' getaways. They spoiled her and made her feel as if she could do no wrong. There was a sense of complete and unconditional love that felt different than any other relationship.

When the reporter ended the report, the camera flashed over the woman with sad eyes. As it did, it felt as if her eyes once again bore into Ashley's. Yes, she must at least look into this. That grandmother deserved to know her granddaughter was safe.

37

ASHLEY

Christmas was only a month away. It would be Ashley's first Christmas without her dad. She and her mom decided to continue their holiday traditions, including baking Christmas cookies, something they'd done as long as she could remember.

As she entered her mom's house, Christmas music filled the air. She caught her breath as a sting filled her eyes. Her dad usually took several weeks off at Christmas. His void felt larger with the holidays.

Ashley and her mom visited as they mixed up sweet treats. Rolling out a sheet of cookies, Ashley half-expected her dad to come whisking into the kitchen. When they baked, he would make frequent trips to check on their progress, sampling the goodies and adding his own advice which included, "Keep trying. They are almost perfect." With a smile and a quick kiss on both his girls' cheeks, he'd be off to his next project or to watch a football game on television. Christmas wouldn't be the same. It wasn't just her dad that filled her mind.

She felt her mom give her a tender hug. Their eyes met and Ashley sighed. Guess she'd gotten lost in her thoughts.

"So, what's caused my beautiful daughter to be so quiet today?"

"Oh, I'm sorry Mom, this is supposed to be a fun time together. I guess I'm feeling melancholy. Missing Dad. Other things..."

"Me too. Want to share?"

She took a deep breath and moved to sit at the table. Her mom followed carrying two mugs of hot chocolate. "It's hard to even find the words."

"Take your time. We have all day."

She took a deep breath, trying to keep her voice from wavering. "Dad was such a good man. I miss him so much. Yet daily, I work with fathers and mothers who don't deserve their children. They are horrible to them. Where is God in the midst of all this suffering?"

Her mom squeezed her hand and nodded for Ashley to continue.

"So many children are suffering. Adults too. A couple weeks ago a grandmother left a note on my windshield. She's lost contact with her granddaughter whom she's raised from birth. I can't imagine how devastated she must feel."

"How did she lose contact?"

"The birth father showed up and wanted the little girl, so she was removed from the grandmother and she hasn't been in contact since."

"Oh, how awful."

"Yes, my heart breaks for her. I tried to do some investigating."

"And?"

"I didn't get too far. The caseworker who has the case wasn't willing to share details with me." She sighed again. "I thought I could help these children, but the more involved I become, the worse it feels. I don't understand how I could be so lucky to be rescued and adopted by you and Dad when so many never get a home. Why did I deserve that more than all these children? Where is God for them?"

"I'm sure you see so much suffering honey. I can't imagine. One thing is certain: God is with those children."

Ashley nodded. Her mom's answer wasn't surprising. Ashley always admired her deep faith, something she'd passed onto Ashley. Yet, at this moment, God seemed far away and distant. When did that happen? Why did it happen?

"Ashley, you are part of God's plan in their lives. It's no accident you chose this field, honey. You are God's hands and feet as you help these little ones deal with the chaos in their lives."

"I don't know. It seems as if I'm not doing enough. This is the hardest time of the year to remove children from their homes. Who really wants to take children away from their family when it's Christmas? Yet, how awful it would be to leave them in unsafe places, just because it's Christmas."

"Those children are so lucky to have you."

Ashley looked at her mom. She shrugged. "Sometimes I wonder..."

"What do you mean honey?" Her mom lifted the hot chocolate to her lips and took a sip as she waited for Ashley to respond.

Ashley did the same. Hot chocolate was one of her favorite comfort foods. It had a magical way of calming her. She took another sip before she responded. "There are such extremes. I have cases where children have been abused or mistreated so horribly, and yet the parents are given numerous chances to continue parenting. Then there are the cases when I question if removing the children and putting them in foster care is in their best interest."

"Like when?"

"Like this last week. Robin handed me a case with specific instructions to remove the children from a home. She already contacted the foster home placement. When I got to the children's home, everything seemed okay. The house was in disarray, but the children looked safe and adequately cared for. I couldn't sense any imminent danger and yet, Robin made it clear I was not to leave the children there. She emphasized it several times when she handed me the file."

"Interesting..."

"Anyway, as I loaded the children into my car, I asked the seven-year-old boy how I could help him. Do you know what he said?"

Her mom shook her head.

"Help my mommy so we don't have to go." Ashley sighed. "Mom, those were the words of a seven-year-old boy!"

Her mom clutched her throat. "How heartbreaking."

"That home might not have been perfect, but it was his home. I'm not sure I did the right thing for those kids."

"Why do you think Robin asked you to do that?" Her mom had a way of asking questions that brought out good discussion.

"I'm not sure, especially once I got to the foster home she'd directed me to. That house was a mess. There must have been ten other kids there. Dirty dishes were stacked on the counter. It smelled filthy. It was worse than the home I'd taken them from."

"How sad."

"I think the mom just needed a hand up. I didn't feel good about taking those children. There has to be a better way." Ashley realized RT's conversation lingered in her mind. "Anyway, after I dropped the children off at the foster home, I went back to the office. I told Robin my concerns. She explained we couldn't leave children in a home where there is a RISK of them being hurt. I have never done a removal with no evidence of neglect or abuse, that was based on a perceived risk alone."

"So, who thought the children were at risk of being hurt?" Her mom seemed confused.

"That's what really bothered me, Mom. Robin told me an ex-boyfriend filed the report."

"What?" Her mom's face paled.

"I got the feeling the ex was being vindictive to cause trouble for that mom. To make her life sad and miserable, especially at Christmas time." Ashley shook her head in disbelief.

Her mom reached to touch Ashley's arm. "What can you do?"

"I don't know. Robin was absolute in her instructions and even though I didn't feel good about it, I didn't want to be fired, but I can't stand the thought of those kids not getting a Christmas gift, so before

I stopped here, I ran to Walmart. I purchased gifts for them, but I wonder if they will even get them."

"Oh honey, how thoughtful. Ashley, you do an amazing job."

"Thanks Mom." She appreciated her mom's support.

"Honey, look at all the children you've helped. Children who are safe because of your work. There might be more to this situation. There has to be good cause for your department to be called. You have good instincts. Follow your gut. It has served you well many times."

"You're probably right Mom. I think I'm emotional and exhausted right now, seeing so many broken homes, missing Dad, the holidays. I don't know, sometimes it seems like life is lopsided to loss and brokenness rather than peace and wholeness."

Her mom nodded. "We do live in a fallen world Ashley. God never intended for there to be loss, death, or sadness, but we all live under the sin of mankind. That's why God sent Jesus to save us from our own brokenness and despair. You do the same for those children."

"What a kind analogy Mom. It really is." She paused to collect herself. "I can't imagine not having you and Dad." Her bottom lip trembled.

"Oh honey. You know your dad and I always believed you were meant to be our child. Just like God took care of you, He will take care of those children. He has a plan for them too, even if we can't see it right now."

"I hope you're right Mom. As I watch these children, I sometimes feel like I'm suffocating. I can't get that single mom out of my mind, or that grandmother who is missing her granddaughter. How horrible Christmas will be for them. I wish there was a better way."

They talked late into the evening. By the time the last sheet of cookies came out of the oven, they were both too tired to decorate them. They could wait until tomorrow.

Ashley and her mom said their goodnights. She'd planned to stay in her childhood room tonight so she could help decorate the house tomorrow. It had been a while since she'd slept here. It might be fun tonight. Her dad might feel a little closer.

As she drifted off to sleep, she thought of how her dad used to tuck her in, pretending to whisper in her ear only to give her a little whisker burn with his 5 o'clock shadow. It always made her giggle. Why couldn't every child have a daddy like the one she'd had?

38

ASHLEY

The next morning, Ashley woke to the sun streaming in the window. How long had she slept? And why in the world did she wake up with RT on her mind?

She made her way to the kitchen. Her mom sat at the table, coffee cup in hand, reading the paper. Ashley greeted her and made her way to the coffee pot. "Any news?" She pointed at the newspaper.

"No, not really." Her mom looked up at her and gave her a warm smile.

"I might have some..."

"Really?" Her mom's eyebrows raised.

"Yes, I don't know why I failed to mention this last night. I guess my mind was on heavier things. I've met a guy."

"REALLY? Tell me more." Her mom's eyes widened, filled with intrigue and her familiar sparkle.

"It's not a big deal, but I like him. He's a defense attorney, of all things."

"Attorneys make good providers." A teasing tone filled her voice.

"Oh Mom, you know that's not my first interest."

"Yes, I do honey. That's why I couldn't resist saying it. So, details please!"

"I probably shouldn't say anything yet. We're just getting to know each other. I don't know if it's even going anywhere, but it is nice to hang out with a man who seems interested in getting to know me. He has a colorful life which has caused me to ponder things about my own life." Ashley could feel a blush coming to her cheeks.

Her mom tipped her head. "Colorful?"

Ashley smiled and shared what she knew about RT. As her mom listened, a growing smile spread across her face. She was always a sap for romance. How many evenings had the two of them sat crying their eyes out over some romantic flick, while her dad went off to his den to watch an action movie? She was glad she mentioned RT. Her mother seemed more relaxed as they chatted about happier subjects.

"He's asked me to come watch him with his next case. He claims to defend the innocent. He said I need to be there."

"So, are you going?"

"I'd like to." Ashley hesitated. "I've discovered I can learn a lot about a person by watching them in action, especially in the courtroom. I've seen so many cases, I've gotten good at seeing the truth. Besides, it's a child welfare case, one I'm not working on. It might be fun to watch a case where I don't already have an opinion about. RT told me this case could cause me to change my profession." She laughed. "Like that will happen!"

"You never know honey. After our conversation last night, maybe you need to look at another line of work. Maybe there is something else you could do to still help children. I sense discontentment growing in you."

Ashley wanted to share that some of the discontentment had to do with her desire to know more about her biological family, but she didn't want to shatter the light mood. She wasn't sure how her mom would feel about it. She paused to gather her thoughts. "You may be right Mom. It's hard watching children being bounced in and out of foster homes while their parents bounce in and out of sobriety. It's so unfair to the children. The parents don't seem to understand that their children are getting attached to other people and feeling torn about their loyalties. It hurts the kids not to have some sort of permanency in their lives."

"They must be so confused."

"Yes, they are. It's hard on them, the foster families, the biological family, and all the extended family, classmates, siblings. It's hard on the whole community who are a part of the children's lives. Sometimes children return to their biological family before the family is ready. Then they end up back in the system. It's exhausting. We are constantly tearing apart and patching together families."

"I worry about you, honey." Her mom patted Ashley's hand.

"Thanks Mom. I'll admit, sometimes I feel traumatized by things I've seen and experienced, and I'm trained to do this work. It's no wonder the children are hurt in this process."

"You care so much about them."

She nodded. "I do. It's a hard job and yet, very rewarding. It's confusing too. Some parents do the bare minimum to get their kids back only to return to destructive habits, yet still keep their kids. Others are genuine, but are given so many stipulations they can't succeed."

"Like what?" Her mom frowned with the question.

"I've seen parenting plans where meetings are stacked on top of each other. How can parents go to multiple meetings at the same time, see their children at scheduled visits, and still hold down a job. They're being set up to fail."

"Oh, that's horrible."

"It is." Ashley took a deep breath. "Maybe I do need to explore other ways to help children."

Her mom watched her closely, but remained quiet.

Ashley looked out the window and then back to her mom. "Oh, for goodness sakes, how did we get on this subject again? If we don't get going on Christmas decorating, we'll never finish."

"We have time. I love hearing you talk about your work. You're so passionate."

"I am, but that doesn't mean we have to talk about it all the time." Her mom's comment made her think of the passion RT had shown during their recent conversation. Maybe she should go see him in action. It would be interesting. Actually, it would be interesting to do most anything with him. She could feel her face blushing at the very thought. She hoped her mom hadn't noticed.

Nothing slipped by her mom though, who smiled as she watched Ashley. "Thinking about that young man again?"

How did her mom do that? It was like she could read her mind. Ashley chuckled. "I must admit, he does give me happier things to ponder."

"You better take him up on his invitation to sit in on his case. I think there's something special there. I haven't seen you like this in a long time." Her mom winked.

"I think I just might."

As they decorated cookies, a lightness filled the air. They were moving on. Her dad would have wanted that.

39

SARAH

Sarah arrived at church. It had become a welcome ritual through the years. Today, the excitement of Christmas just weeks away made it extra special. White lights decorated the church along with a large Christmas tree that sat off to one side. Wreaths and poinsettias were scattered about.

This church held memories. She and Tyler baptized all three of their children here. Noah's funeral was here. As a young family, the children attended Sunday school while she and Tyler sat in the hard pews, holding hands, happy to have some time without the children. Sunday school meant a break for mom and dad while the kids attended their classes. Sarah smiled thinking of those times when Tyler was close by her side.

She remembered how eager the children had been to share songs and Bible verses they learned. The car seemed to bounce as they left the church parking lot, singing Jesus Loves Me at the top of their lungs.

Sundays werc their special day. Sometimes she would pack a picnic and they'd go to the park and play, or they'd stop at the grocery store and pick up a candy bar, a rare treat. On even rarer occasions, they would stop at the drive in and order burgers and fries. She loved the day to unwind, play board games, and take leisurely walks.

After her life fell apart, she found it difficult to return to church, but over time, this became the place she felt most at peace. Here she allowed herself the treasure of friends. Many of the casseroles that arrived on her doorstep were from women at this church. When her car broke down or the plumbing backed up, members of this church lent a helping hand. She felt indebted to them for their willingness to stand in the gap through the years.

This was also the place where she cried out to God, shaking her fist and demanding answers. She threatened and cursed Him, and tried to bribe Him with words like, "If only you'll bring my children back, then I'll..." In the end, when no answers came, this is where she learned that in her brokenness, she was accepted and loved.

As the years passed, she found meaning here in helping others who went through trials. Despite her years as a churchgoer, she hadn't come to terms with what religion meant to her. She knew God was real. She knew Noah was in heaven. She believed someday she would see her son again. Decades of unanswered questions left her wondering. Did miracles still happen? Were prayers still answered?

A little girl jostled next to her. It jarred Sarah from her memories. She turned to smile. "You look so beautiful."

The little girl smiled back as she smoothed her lace dress with the velvet bow. It reminded Sarah of the dress she'd purchased for Leanna that last Christmas before she was taken. It amazed her how, after all these years, such a simple thing like a little girl's Christmas dress could freshen her grief. It would come at the most unexpected times, but there was comfort in the pain. It reminded her that no amount of time could separate her heart from them, even if they were only a memory. Sarah took a deep breath and allowed her shoulders to relax. Yes, in spite of the multitude of memories that paraded through her head, this was a wonderful place to be.

When the pastor came to the pulpit, he led them in vigorous worship. She felt her heart swell with emotion. She loved to sing. It felt good to focus on worshiping God. After several songs, the pastor started his sermon.

"Please open your Bibles to Philippians 1:22-26 from the Message translation, let's read together. *'As long as I'm alive in this body, there is good work for me to do. If I had to choose right now, I hardly know which I'd choose. Hard choice! The desire to break camp here and be with Christ is powerful. Some days I can think of nothing better. But most days, because of what you are going through, I am sure that it's better for me to stick it out here. So I plan to be around awhile, companion to you as your growth and joy in this life of trusting God continues. You can start looking forward to a great reunion when I come visit you again. We'll be praising Christ, enjoying each other.'* My friends, isn't this scripture so true today? Isn't the work of this life hard? And if given the choice, wouldn't some of us be ready to be with Christ?"

"Hard" didn't cover what she'd been dealt, but she didn't let her mind wander as she continued to listen to the pastor: "Paul reminds us that each day we're given is a gift. With that gift, there is work to do. What work does God have for you to do? Since you're still on this earth, you're not finished. It doesn't matter if you've retired from a wonderful career or are so young you don't know what you're going to do yet. You're alive, so that means you still have work to do, work to do for the Lord. That's why we're here, to be of service to our Lord."

Sarah wondered what work God still had for her to do. She loved her work at the hospital with the older folks, but there was a void. Being a mother was the role she felt God really intended for her.

The pastor continued. "Paul's message has another promise. Paul wrote that we can all look forward to a great reunion. He was referring to his return to his friends, but we can also anticipate a great reunion with Christ."

"You'll have a great reunion too, my daughter." The words were as clear as day yet felt as if they had been whispered into her soul. That never happened before. She looked around to see if anyone else heard, but everyone seemed to be focused on the pastor. An incredible peace settled over her. She felt a sense of exhilaration.

Without a doubt, she knew she'd just heard the still small voice of God.

She didn't know what to make of it as tears flowed down her cheeks. She wiped them away. When the service wrapped up, she felt as if she had a special secret. She wanted to share it, but it wasn't the kind of thing everyone would understand. In fact, some might think she'd lost her mind. So, she went to the one place where she could talk most freely; Noah's grave. She visited every month. It was the last connection to her family of the past.

As Sarah stepped out of her car, the winter air chilled her. She pulled her coat closer. Nearing the grave, she knelt to clear away the dead grass. She'd brought fresh yellow daisies and laid them on the headstone. They wouldn't last long in this temperature, but she brought them every time she came. They made her think of him. She smiled, remembering his sweet innocence on the day he'd waddled over and handed her a handful of mashed daisies. When she looked over his shoulder, she saw what remained of her flower bed. It was completely thrashed, but she couldn't be mad. It had been such a tender gesture. After all these years, it still warmed her heart.

She knelt to sit on the ground, hardened from the frost. It made her think of how she hardened some through the years, but today she felt different. It felt as if her heart was thawing, like God had given her a promise, a glorious reunion. She shared her secret with Noah, along with other matters of her heart.

After a time, she felt a chill. Glancing to the sky, she realized the clouds now covered the sun. Picking herself up from the ground, she placed a kiss on Noah's headstone and whispered, "I love you, Noah. See you next month, my sweet baby."

40

ASHLEY

Ashley arrived at the courtroom early. She'd requested the day off so she could observe RT's trial. She needed a break. Between conversations with RT, her desire to know more about her biological family, missing her dad, the holidays, and her work concerns, she needed time to think. The courtroom might not be the best place, but it would provide a good distraction.

Court hadn't been called into session so she found herself thinking of RT. In the months since they met, they continued to get together. Sometimes they took a short walk around the courthouse during a break. Other times they met for coffee at the coffee shop down the street. He continued to share his desire to help wrongly accused parents and she continued to share her passion to protect children. Yet, romantically, their relationship was going nowhere. As much as she enjoyed his company, like other men she'd dated, something was missing. Why couldn't she seem to connect romantically, especially with him?

She also hadn't gotten around to telling him she had been a foster kid. She wasn't keeping it a secret. It's just there were always other things to talk about. For now, being his friend felt safe and comfortable. After this case, perhaps they would have a better understanding of where their relationship might go.

As the judge slammed down the gavel, Ashley jerked in her seat. Once again, her head was in the clouds thinking about him rather than the proceedings in the courtroom. Getting her mind back into the moment, she had her first opportunity to see RT's client Bob. He was young, handsome and clean-cut. A young woman sat right behind him, perhaps his wife?

As the trial proceeded, she could see why this young man had gotten under RT's skin. He didn't seem like most fathers she met. Some of them didn't even bother to show up for court. As she watched Bob, he reminded her of a younger version of her own dad. She hoped that wouldn't taint her judgment. She wanted to be objective since anything said in the courtroom could be discussed the next time she met with RT. She wondered when that might be. Perhaps even this week? This case would make for very interesting conversation.

RT presented his opening statement with confidence. He explained an accident happened, causing Bob's son to be injured. It was not a criminal or intentional act that warranted jail or even condemnation, but rather an accident.

As more details were shared, she watched Bob struggle to maintain his composure, as did the woman sitting behind him. Ashley felt drawn to them and her heart broke for what this family endured. She also found herself drawn to RT and the clear passion for his work. His presentation came across as credible and persuasive. It reminded her of the first time she saw him in court, the day that led to their first date.

The judge seemed unaffected by RT. She noted the familiar flat look in the judge's eyes. He ruled on many of her cases and could be especially hard on fathers. Perhaps he had grown calloused after hearing so many stories and excuses from deadbeat dads.

As witnesses were called forth, she found herself sympathizing with Bob. How could a father prevent every accident that happens to their children? Why would he be held responsible? Most parents do the best they can to protect their children. Those who don't are obvious. The signs are everywhere; unexplained bruises, unattended injuries, missing school, lack of attention to medical issues, malnutrition, and deviant behavior.

This father had done everything opposite. He had taken his child to the emergency room, detailing every bump and bruise. He wasn't hiding anything as he tried to help his son. If all fathers were this passionate about their children's health and well-being, she wouldn't have a job. A chill ran down her spine. Isn't that what RT had been trying to tell her? Thankfully there were caseworkers to advocate for abused and neglected children, but had the agency overreached to justify jobs or worse yet, for financial gain?

When the judge called a lunch recess, Ashley's mind whirled. In the hundreds of cases she'd worked on, she never experienced this feeling. She knew she had a good sense of judgment. That's what made her so good at what she did. So why did this feel so wrong, and why such a sense of injustice? Perhaps her friendship with RT clouded her judgment, but this couple seemed so much different than parents she'd worked with. Perhaps there really was something very wrong with this case.

41

RT

As RT closed his briefcase and headed down the center aisle toward the back door, he saw Ashley out of the corner of his eye. His heart skipped a beat. She made it. He couldn't believe it. As his eyes met hers, she smiled. It made him suck in his breath.

Ashley spoke first. "Hey, pretty impressive in there." She nodded toward the front of the room.

"Thank you." A smile tugged at the corner of his mouth. He wasn't comfortable with compliments, but it pleased him. Actually, he was most pleased she'd decided to come to court to hear about his case.

"Any chance you'd like to grab lunch?"

He glanced at his watch and grimaced. "Oh, I wish."

The sparkle in her eyes dimmed. He could see her disappointment, but as much as he'd like to have lunch, he couldn't take time off now. He needed to prepare and based on how he was reading the judge, he had a full afternoon ahead of him. In fact, he'd be lucky to even get to bed tonight. He couldn't let Bob down.

"It's okay." She squeezed his arm.

"I'd really like to. Could we take a rain check?"

"That would be great. We'll do it soon."

He put his arm around her shoulder and gave her a slight hug. "Thank you so much for coming. I really appreciate it, and I do want to get together. Maybe next week?"

"That sounds great." Her eyes lingered.

RT's gaze lingered. Wow, what beautiful blue eyes.

A curious look came over her face. "Are you okay?"

"Oh yes. I'm sorry. Have I ever told you what beautiful eyes you have?"

She blushed. "Actually, you haven't, but thank you."

His heart hammered. He wondered if she could hear it. She was a stunning woman. Once he wrapped up this case, he needed to make the next move with her. He pulled her back into his embrace and whispered in her ear. "Thank you again. I look forward to our rain check."

With that he released her and turned to walk away. He'd better put some distance between himself and this beautiful lady if he intended to get any work done today.

42

ASHLEY

As Ashley left the courthouse, she felt renewed from RT's hug. And his whisper in her ear, was he flirting with her? She smiled. Perhaps as adversaries, they might have found common ground.

She decided the time had come to share the story of her past. In fact, it was time for her to figure it out herself. She thought of the warehouse that held all the old CPS records. With the rest of the day off, perhaps she could get into the warehouse and look for some answers. The guards wouldn't question her being there as an employee, and since she'd taken the day off, Robin wouldn't need to know either.

Ashley slipped her hand into her purse. She felt her state ID. She would need that to gain access to the warehouse. She reminded herself she could get fired for this, but she needed to know. Discussions with her mom hadn't brought forth any new information. If she wanted answers, she had no other choice.

Adoption cases this old were sometimes difficult to find, but her odds were better than most. She knew her birth date, where she was born, and the general time of the adoption.

She pulled into the parking lot and flashed her ID at the security officer. He waved her through. As she walked toward the warehouse, she could feel her heart pounding. She had only been in this building one other time when she accompanied a clerk to bring records here for storage.

She opened the door and reached into the dark, sliding her hand up against the wall. When she located the light switch, she turned it on. Taking time for her eyes to adjust, she surveyed the long rows of shelves. She started walking the aisles until she found boxes dated the year her adoption had been finalized. That is when her case would have been closed.

The shelves were piled high with boxes. The light was dim, but the small flashlight she carried in her purse proved to be helpful. When she saw the number of boxes with that date range, her heart sank. You'd think in this age of technology, things would be more organized. In fact, you'd think these records would be computerized. Then again, who would have time to do that? They were too busy trying to keep up with the needs of the children and filling out more paperwork.

She noticed her hands were sweaty even though the warehouse was cool. A shiver ran down her spine as once again, she thought of the trouble she could get in for doing this. She took a deep breath. She was here now, might as well get to work. She just hoped in these mounds of boxes, she could find something helpful, and if she did, she hoped she could handle whatever she learned.

43

TYLER

Bob looked tired when he came back to the cell after his day in court.

Tyler patted him on the back. "How'd it go?"

Bob shook his head. "It's still early. I'm confident my attorney will get the facts out."

"You're pretty sure of that attorney you have."

Bob nodded. "Yes, I am."

Tyler couldn't help thinking of his own attorney who had been such a disappointment. "You sure this guy is going to take care of you?"

"Yes. He believes in my innocence, and he's smart, but it's going to be harder than I thought." Bob sat on his cot, clasped his hands together, and rested his forehead on them.

Even though Tyler's trial had been over twenty-four years ago, the memory of it was etched in his mind. He remembered the feeling of getting beaten down after listening to testimony that made him feel unworthy as a father, let alone as a man. What kind of man let his own child die? He remembered the damning words of the prosecutor and how forcefully he pointed his finger at Tyler during closing arguments. He remembered how the prosecutor demanded justice for Noah, and how the jury glared at him, as if he deliberately killed his son. He knew they were going to convict him.

That was when he made the decision to take the plea. Twenty-five years sounded better than life in prison, but prison was nothing compared to the punishment he got. Not a day passed when he didn't blame himself for Noah's death or what it cost his whole family.

Bob spoke. It startled him. So lost in thought, he'd forgotten they were having a conversation. "I'm sorry. What did you say?" He felt embarrassed he hadn't heard Bob, just two feet away. Talk about looking like an old man who'd lost his hearing.

Bob stood and raised his voice. "Are you okay? You look like you're lost!"

"Oh. No, I'm fine."

"So, are you okay with that?" Bob looked as if he expected an answer.

Tyler realized he hadn't been listening. "I guess I didn't hear what you said."

"I said, I hope you don't mind, but I've asked my attorney to make time to meet you the next time he's here."

Tyler let out an exasperated sigh. "I doubt it would do any good."

Bob put his arm around Tyler's shoulder. "Trust me. You need to meet him."

The word trust lobbed off Tyler's mind. Odd as it seemed, in the short time they had been stuck in this cell, he had come to trust Bob. That was rare in prison, but he'd been watching Bob for months now. He never failed to get out of bed, get on his knees, and whisper prayers each and every morning. He was as trustworthy as the sun itself. As time passed, Bob never seemed to get discouraged. Instead, his confidence grew. He had a quiet, peaceful spirit. He still hadn't shown any anger.

Tyler thought back to the anger he'd felt after his conviction. His rage consumed him. He'd acted out in violence and ultimately, he withdrew. Bob seemed to be at total peace. Perhaps it had something to do with his faith. It seemed personal, like God was right there in the cell. His prayers were passionate and intimate, nothing like the rote prayers Tyler had been taught.

"So, you'll meet him?" Bob didn't know the meaning of giving up.

Tyler took a deep breath. "Yes, I'll meet him. Now can we stop talking about it?"

Bob smiled. He didn't say another word.

*   *   *   *   *

Early the next morning, Tyler watched Bob get out of bed and kneel on the floor, just like every other morning. Tyler felt an odd sense of being left out, like there was some sort of meeting taking place in his own cell that he hadn't been invited to. His curiosity got the best of him. "Why do you pray to a god that allowed you to go to prison for something you didn't do?"

Bob was quiet for a moment. "Because I trust Him."

Tyler rolled his eyes.

Bob didn't seem to notice. "Just because I'm locked in here doesn't mean he's locked out. He's here too."

Tyler clamped his mouth shut. He wished he hadn't asked. He certainly didn't want to tell Bob how nuts that sounded.

Bob continued. "You know Tyler, I'm not the first man in history to serve time as an innocent man, and to be honest, this prison is really a blessing compared to the prisons others are in."

"What do you mean?" As soon as he'd asked the question, Tyler regretted it. Why ask questions that would keep this crazy conversation going?

Bob continued without missing a beat. "People build their own prisons all the time. Addictions keep them locked away from reality and the people who want to help them. Some people build emotional walls to hide their feelings, pushing away others, even their own families. At least here, there's no question what is separating me from those I love." He pulled on the cell bars.

Bob's words hit a chord. He thought of Sarah and emotions began to rise. He had done that to her, to himself by pushing her away, locking her out of his life. "Guess I never thought about it that way."

Bob had more to say. "God has always been in here with me. He knows I'm innocent and no matter what happens, I trust Him to the outcome." He paused, then continued. "Tyler, look at me." Tyler lifted his eyes to look at Bob. "God knows you're innocent too."

Tyler couldn't explain the rush of emotion he was experiencing. He could feel his eyes stinging. He brushed the backside of his hand against his eyes to keep tears from erupting and said the first thing that came to his mind. "It didn't do me any good." His voice sounded rough with an edge of anger.

Bob didn't take his eyes off Tyler's face. He allowed silence to soothe the moment. Then he spoke again. "God isn't done writing your story Tyler. He's never forgotten you're here. You haven't had an easy road, but it's not the end. God will use our circumstances for something good. Satan is the one who wanted us to be in this prison, not God. What the enemy intends for harm and destruction, God will use for good."

"How can you be so certain? Besides, I gave up on God years ago. I doubt he's interested in helping me now."

Bob put his hand on Tyler's shoulder. "From what you've shared with me, it sounds like you haven't heard from your family in years."

Tyler nodded as a lump grew in his throat.

Bob continued. "Which one of your family members would you refuse to see after all these years?"

He gulped. His voice quivered. "I'd give anything to see any of them."

"That's how God feels about you Tyler. Not only would He give anything, He gave everything, including His own son. He wants to have a relationship with you. Even though you gave up on Him, He's never given up on you." Bob's words came out in a whisper.

A sense of reverence and peace filled the cell. It made Tyler's hair stand on end. He didn't want to breathe for fear it would dissipate.

"Can you feel Him, Tyler? Can you feel His love, His presence here?" His voice was barely audible.

Tyler nodded.

"He's waiting for you, Tyler. He wants to be in your life, but he loves you too much to barge in uninvited. Are you ready to invite him in?"

His throat felt tight. His heart raced. He nodded yes.

Bob put his arm around his shoulder and began praying. "Jesus, thank you for coming to us since, without you, we can't come to you. Thank you for loving us so much that you gave up everything, including your life. Through your gift, we acknowledge we can be called your sons. We accept your gift, Lord. We ask you to be the Lord of our lives. Please direct our paths so that we may honor you with the days you have given us. Amen."

A solemn stillness filled the air. Tyler wanted to bask in it. The silence lingered, then Bob stepped back to look in Tyler's eyes. "You know Tyler, if for no other reason than a chance to pray with you, I'm glad God allowed me to be in prison. It is an honor my brother."

With that, years of hardened emotion came crashing down like sheets of glacial ice falling into the ocean. Tyler knew he would never be the same.

44

ASHLEY

Ashley had been at the warehouse for about an hour, opening dusty lids and peering inside, searching for information that matched hers. Discouragement edged into her mind. Opening another box, she caught her breath. Her birth date was printed on the top page. She glanced down the sheet and read the name, Leanna Thornton. Dang. This wasn't her file. Just as she started to close the box, she noticed the adoption date. It was in the same timeframe as hers. Maybe?

Taking the box from the shelf, she felt excitement and trepidation at the same time. She glanced around and noticed an empty table nearby. She carried the box to it and set it down. Removing the file from the box, she took care to leave a space so she could put the file back in the right place. As she scanned through the first few pages, she couldn't seem to keep her emotions in check. There was no reason to believe this might be her family and yet, just maybe?

She read the parents' names: Tyler and Sarah Thornton. That didn't strike a chord of recollection. She read on. The names of the children, Ryan age 7, Leanna age 2 1/2, Noah deceased at age 18 months. How sad. If this had been her family, then she would have brothers. Then again, this probably wasn't her file. Yet, given the dates and now the age that matched when she went into foster care, perhaps? It felt like being on a mental yoyo.

Ashley paused to take a breath. She had to be careful not to make something hers that wasn't. Yet, she couldn't help getting excited. She flipped to another page and read about how Tyler had been found guilty of negligent homicide and child neglect. Her heart sank. If this was her family, then her father neglected her, just as she always assumed.

Taking her time, not wanting to misinterpret anything, she read through the pages. Little Noah's death, such a tragedy. If this was her little brother, why didn't she have any recollection of him, or of her older brother for that matter? Was it possible the trauma of it all blocked her memory? Or maybe she was just too small to remember. Maybe this wasn't her family. Goodness, how quickly she got caught up speculating.

She continued to turn the pages. She read the caseworker notes: "Family referred by local hospital. Death of the 18-month-old son is questionable. Awaiting the coroner's report, but to protect surviving children, CPS removed them from the home. There were notes from the doctor that made the situation seem ominous. Ashley paused as she read them. Would she, as a caseworker, have found this valid? Would she have felt the urgency to remove the children, based on the notes the doctor wrote? She felt a knot growing in her stomach. She read of the mother's distress and hysteria. Public officials questioned whether she could take care of her two children without the father, since he awaited his trial. Such a sad story.

Ashley needed to take a break. This was harder than she thought. She felt like she intruded on a family's private matter and had no business reading this. She flipped to close the file, but the last page stuck to the folder. Glancing down, she read: Leanna adopted by Tom and Rebecca Anderson. She gasped and grabbed the edge of the table to steady herself. The walls of the room felt like they were closing in. Against all odds, she held her own file in her hands, filled with details of her family. She couldn't believe it.

Ashley felt a cold sweat sticking to her skin. She was breathing too fast and needed to calm down. She found a chair, blew off the dust and sat. Who cared if there was dust on the back of her navy slacks?

Her hands shook as she placed them over the cool pages that lay in front of her. She knew she must start over and read each and every word. They would mean something different now that she knew it contained her history.

She thought of her name. Leanna. Why the name change? She'd have to ask her mom. Thoughts of her mom pulled her mind away from the file. She felt like she was betraying her to even be here, looking into her past, but she needed answers. To have found her file seemed to confirm it was time. That was a miracle in itself.

She flipped back to the beginning of the file, grabbed her cell phone, and took pictures of every page. She needed to be able to read this later when she wasn't feeling like she would hyperventilate. She scanned the pages, wanting to pick up the high points. When she read notes about the removal, she slowed her pace. "Children were removed from their home. Mother resisted and had to be restrained. Ryan was aggressive and had to be sedated at the clinic. Initial health assessment - Excellent. Leanna had to be separated from her brother to calm her. Initial health assessment - Excellent."

As she read the words, it occurred to Ashley this is what happened to her, to her brother, and to her mom. A tear fell on the aged paper. She sniffed and wiped her face. She didn't want to damage the pages. Pulling a Kleenex from her purse, she blew her nose and took a deep breath. She would need some time to get through this. She continued reading. "Ryan was placed in a temporary group home. Will locate foster family in the next week, if possible. Leanna was placed with foster/adoptive parents Tom and Becky Anderson."

Pages of records on the progress of the placements followed: "Ryan has become violent and angry. He will remain in the group home until treatment is determined. Leanna is adjusting well to foster home. Andersons have indicated they are willing to adopt."

As she continued to read, a pit grew in her stomach. "Ryan and Leanna met with Sarah. Visit went well but Leanna became upset so the visit was cut short. Ryan continues to act out. Future visits will be separate since Ryan upsets Leanna. Sarah interacted well with children, but doesn't seem to be coping well. Question whether she is capable of parenting. When the children asked of their daddy, Sarah gave inappropriate responses for the age of the children."

Thoughts tumbled through Ashley's mind. *"Of course, little Ryan was acting out. Of course, it upset his two-year-old sister and obviously, Sarah wasn't coping well. Who would, given what she was going through?"*

Her mouth felt dry and she could feel her stomach tightening as she clenched the papers in her hands. Where were the people who should have been helping her family? Where were the compassionate workers who should have supported them? It almost seemed like they were discrediting the family, looking for an excuse to tear them apart.

She began to read of her father's trial. It was almost more than she could comprehend as she skimmed over the notes. "Tyler continues to deny any responsibility. The District Attorney intends to pursue a maximum sentence. Tyler took a plea agreement. Judge sentenced the neglectful father to twenty-five years." She couldn't read any more.

She pushed her chair away from the table. Over two hours passed since she'd entered the warehouse. Her body felt stiff as if wound tightly onto a spring. Ashley needed to take a break, but she did not dare stop as there would likely be no chance to look at this file again. She stood, stretched her back, and continued taking pictures of the pages without reading them. It would be impossible to mentally process this all at once anyway.

As fast as possible, she flipped through the pages and snapped pictures of each one. A phrase caught her attention and she paused. "Parental rights terminated". She'd seen that on other files before. She'd written it herself a number of times, but when she read those words about her own family, it felt like her heart would break. These were the words that set the course for little Ryan, herself, and her parents, changing their world forever. Their past had been dealt a deadly blow. They would never be a family again.

She had to focus. She needed to get through this. She picked up the pace as she continued taking pictures. As she neared the end of the file, she felt nervous. What if someone came to check on her? She needed to get this box back on the shelf. With regret and a sense of longing, she carefully put the files back in the box, put the box back on the shelf, turned out the light, and left the warehouse. She would have liked to take the whole file with her, but that would really be pushing her luck.

She got into her car, feeling as if she had just gotten away with something illegal. She gripped the steering wheel in her hands. It helped her to feel grounded as chaos swirled in her head. Even though the temperature outside was chilly, the inside of the car had become warm from the sun. It felt good compared to the chill of the warehouse. She leaned her head against the side window and soaked in the warmth. She just sat, thinking, and letting herself feel. Had it not been for the security officer knocking on her car window, she might have remained that way all afternoon.

*   *   *   *   *

When Ashley arrived back at her apartment, she turned on her computer and began downloading her camera. Once the pictures downloaded, she printed them off. She would create her own file and find out for herself what happened to her family. There would be no sleep for her tonight.

Seeing her original birth certificate was sobering. Her original name, right there with the names of her biological parents, yet complete strangers to her. What an odd feeling. Turning the page, she searched for an explanation as to why her family became involved with CPS. It must have had something to do with her little

8

brother's death. What caused the death? Aw, yes: "Secondary drowning. Father charged with negligent homicide. Children taken into protective custody until it is determined if they are safe."

Late into the early morning hours, she read details of the trial, conviction, and termination of parental rights. She realized Noah's death, a tragic accident, is what set the wheels in motion. Just like RT's client Bob, her own father was fingered as neglectful for not preventing the accident. That's why it's called an accident. It couldn't have been helped. How horrendous it must have been for her father, to not only deal with his son's death, but also be put on trial and convicted of causing it. How would anyone ever get over that, or even live through it?

Tears started to form in the corners of her eyes. She thought of all the years when, not knowing the facts, she assumed her parents had been neglectful or abusive, such a horrible assumption that now proved to be wrong. She could see how it happened, how the deck had been stacked against them, and how no one helped them in their crisis.

Another thought entered her mind and with it, a chill ran down her spine. Could they have been a victim of government overreach or corruption as RT suggested? Why else would they have been treated so unfairly? The only thing that seemed certain was that during a time of terrific tragedy, they had been forced to relinquish their surviving children. She couldn't imagine anything more horrifying.

45

ASHLEY

Ashley stirred as the sun poked its head above the horizon. Fragments of her dream were still on her mind, not just any dream, the one that replayed through her nighttime thoughts for years. She never understood it.

She lifted her head and rubbed her eyes. She saw the pages on the kitchen table and realized she'd fallen asleep here. Half way between sleep and wake, Ashley tried to sort out the details of her dream; the face of a kind and gentle man whose eyes filled with love, as he lifted her high above his head. The sound of his laughter mixed with her giggles.

Although she'd probably dreamt that more than a hundred times in her life, she could never put it together. Who was he? Perhaps her biological father, an uncle, or friend? Maybe a scene from a movie. She realized he might not even be a real person.

Baffled and unable to come up with answers, she turned her attention to the papers in front of her. The previous day's discovery returned to her mind. It was surreal. She felt a new sense of urgency to learn more, but first she needed to talk to her mom. She glanced at the clock. She'd have to hurry if she was going to stop at her mom's house before work.

After showering, she put her hair in a ponytail, dashed some makeup across her face, and grabbed her purse. Once she arrived at her mom's, she ran up the sidewalk and let herself in and called out: "Mom. Mom. I need to talk to you."

Her mom came around the corner from the kitchen, her forehead pinched in concern. "What is it honey? Is something wrong? Don't you have to work today?"

Ashley wrapped her arms around her mom and hugged her tight. Her mom returned the hug. "Ashley, are you okay?"

"Mom, I have to tell you something." Her words came out in breathless gasps. "It's important. Please forgive me if this causes you any pain, but I had to know." Her heart raced. She sat down hard on the couch and patted the seat next to her.

Her mom sat. Her eyes were wide with worry. "Know what?"

Ashley took a deep breath. There was no going back. "About my biological family."

Her mom's eyes softened. "Oh honey, what did you learn?"

"Please know I believe you and Dad are gifts to me. I would never change that, but I discovered something rather unsettling."

"Tell me." She pulled Ashley's hand into hers.

"I will, but first, can you tell me why my name is Ashley?"

Her mom nodded. "When you first came to us, you called yourself Lee. Although we knew your name was Leanna, I always planned to name my little girl Ashley, after my best friend. So, when we finalized the adoption, we legally changed your name to Ashley. It seemed like an easy switch since you were already calling yourself Lee. Over time, you picked up the whole name."

"It's odd we never talked about it."

"I'm sorry. I didn't know how much to tell you since it could have opened up other questions that I didn't have answers for. I'm sorry Ashley."

"It's okay Mom. I understand. I hope my search hasn't hurt you in any way."

"Oh, it hasn't. I've wondered about your biological family too. I figured someday we would have this conversation. To be honest I'm not surprised. You've been asking more questions lately and I figured you were wanting to learn more."

"Yes, I have." She took a breath as she tried to stop her lip from quivering. "Do you think Dad would have been upset?"

"Of course not. Your dad and I spoke about learning about your biological family. He hoped he could help you when you were ready..." Her voice trailed off.

Ashley squeezed her mom's hand. "I wish he were here too." A husky sensation settled in her throat. She swallowed hard. "Mom, it appears my biological family..." She paused. "They were not abusive or neglectful. I can't be certain, but I don't think they were treated right. I think CPS took me and my brother when they shouldn't have."

"You have a brother?" Her mom's eyes widened as she put her hand over her mouth.

"Yes, two of them. One died. That appears to be what started their involvement with CPS."

"Oh, my goodness. I had no idea. I wish we would have known. Your dad and I would have been willing to take another child, especially if it was your sibling, but back up. What were you saying about them? That they weren't abusive? And a brother died?"

"It all sounds so tragic Mom. I don't understand it yet, but I feel such sadness for what they went through and yet, grateful I was raised by you and Dad." She stopped to look in her mom's eyes. "I'm so conflicted."

Her mom nodded. "So, what now Ashley? Do you want to find them?"

"I don't know. They may not be alive, and if they are, perhaps it would be too painful for them to dig all this up. I've heard of situations where reunions don't go well. I don't know if I can take that level of rejection."

"That would be very difficult and yet, I sense you need to know."

She hesitated before speaking again. Her words came out filled with sorrow, "I do and yet, I feel ashamed."

"Why, honey?"

"For years I thought so poorly of them. I thought they must have been terrible people to have allowed me to be taken from them."

Her mom pulled her close and kissed her cheek. "Honey, everything is going to be okay. This is new to both of us. You don't need to decide anything today. Let's both pray about it, and give this some time. I know God will give you, or rather, us direction."

"You're right Mom." She glanced at her watch. "Oh, my goodness. Look at the time. I better get to work. We can visit more later, but I had to talk to you. Are you sure you're okay?"

"Yes, absolutely. What about you? Are you okay?"

"Don't worry Mom. I'm fine. I'm actually relieved. It's nice to know more about them, and about who I am." She sighed.

Her mom smiled. "Oh, that's something I've never wondered about. You've always been the light of our lives and no matter what, you will always be. And trust me, your dad would have been fine with this."

"I hope so. I love you both so much." She gave her mom a hug.

"Ashley, you do what's right for you. No matter what, I support your decision, and if finding your family turns out to be hurtful, at least you'll know. We have each other. Nothing will ever change that."

"Thanks for understanding."

"I'll be anxious to hear what you decide. Let me know how I can help."

She gave her mom one last hug, pulled the door shut, and headed for her car. She felt a lightness in her step as relief swept over her. She was anxious to continue her search, and God willing, she would find her family.

*   *   *   *   *

Ashley's day was packed from the moment she arrived at work. Probably a good thing. It kept her from focusing on what was really on her mind, her own family. She couldn't wait to get back to her computer and continue her search. Once home, she grabbed a protein bar and went straight to her computer. She began searching for their names. Hours passed. She hadn't learned much. She couldn't even find the names Sarah or Ryan Thornton. It was as if they'd dropped off the edge of the earth. How could there be no mention of either of them? It didn't make sense. Granted there wasn't the internet or Google back then, but you'd have to be a recluse to not have your name appear somewhere. Or dead.

Sadness filled her as that thought popped into her mind. Twenty-five years was a long time. Anything could have happened. She'd heard of parents who took their own lives when they lost their children, a loss they couldn't bear. Perhaps that happened to her family. It would have been a horrific thing to live through.

Even though she hadn't found anything on Sarah or Ryan, she found an article about Tyler. The headlines caused a chill to run down her spine. "Local Man Admits Negligence in Death of Toddler Son." A knot formed in her stomach as she read the story. This was her father, a man who spent twenty-five years in prison, twenty-five years away from his family. That was a lifetime, hers anyway.

She wondered how different her life might have been with Sarah and Tyler as her parents. What would it have been like to have an older brother instead of being an only child, or living in the shadow of her little brother's death? She wondered if Tyler was still in prison. If so, he should be getting close to the end of his sentence. Perhaps he'd been paroled early. How could she find out? She wondered if he'd be receptive to meeting? It made her nervous and excited at the same time.

She wondered if she looked like any of them. It would be odd to look like someone. She didn't resemble either of her parents. Did she have any extended family? Maybe her brother was married with a family and thus she'd have nieces or nephews, but she was getting ahead of herself. One step at a time. Find them first. See where it goes. Her brother might not want anything to do with her. She had to prepare herself for that possibility.

As she shut the computer off for the night, her mind wouldn't quiet enough to consider sleep. She wished she had learned more. If she could find Tyler, maybe he would know about Ryan and Sarah. It was a start. Maybe it wouldn't be as daunting as it felt right now.

46

RT

Bob and RT had a lot to do in the next hour to prepare for his trial. After strategizing together, the guard brought Bob back to his cell. RT remained in the interview room. He agreed to meet with Bob's cell mate. The meeting had been arranged for today.

RT was jotting down notes when the door opened. He lifted his eyes from the notepad to see Tyler enter. Catching his eye, he felt a chill run down his spine. There was something about this guy. Ignoring the unsettled feeling, he stood to greet him, extending his hand, "RT Ellington. It's nice to meet you."

"Nice to meet you too." Tyler returned the handshake. "I'm grateful you're willing to visit with me. Bob speaks highly of you."

"Thank you. Have a chair." He motioned toward the chair on the other side of the table. He was pretty good at reading people. Something wasn't right. RT felt a bit disconnected as he watched Tyler, trying to figure out what sent his senses into overdrive. Then it occurred to him. Tyler looked familiar. But why? From where?

Tyler cleared his throat. "Sir, are you okay?"

RT realized Tyler had been talking to him and yet, he hadn't heard a word. He couldn't seem to connect the dots. Where did he know this guy from? He tried to refocus. "Huh, yes. I'm sorry. Please continue." How embarrassing that he'd lost his focus.

"As I was saying, I'll be getting out of prison in a few weeks and Bob suggested I visit with you. He thought you might be able to help me."

RT continued watching Tyler's expressions. His eyes narrowed as he analyzed his features. Tyler's words were now slow and halted. Realizing he still hadn't absorbed much of what Tyler said, RT interrupted. "I'm sorry. Let's start at the beginning. I usually like to get some basics on my clients before we start into the details of the case. What did you say your name is?" He grabbed his pen and pad and prepared to take notes.

"Tyler. Tyler Thornton."

RT's head jerked up and his mouth flew open. He could feel the blood draining from his face as a bead of sweat made a prickly drip down his neck.

Tyler stared at him with a look of bewilderment. "Have I said something wrong? Perhaps this wasn't a good idea." His chair scraped the floor as he stood and turned to make his way to the door.

"NO!" It came out with more force than RT intended.

Tyler was already moving toward the door; his eyes wide as he put distance between himself and RT.

"I'm sorry. Please. Don't go. I didn't mean to startle you. Please, allow me to explain."

Tyler looked back and forth between RT and the door. His eyes squinted as if to evaluate the situation. He stood partway between the table and the door.

RT took a deep breath and cleared his throat, trying to regain his composure. "When you came in, you looked so familiar. I was having a hard time concentrating while you were talking. Bob told me your name was Tyler." He paused. His next words came out in a raspy breath. "I had no idea it was you."

"What are you talking about?" Tyler continued to keep his distance.

"It's me. Ryan. Your son."

Tyler took a step toward the table, reaching for a chair to steady himself as his knees nearly gave out. RT stepped to his side, steadying him. Both men stared at each other in a state of shock.

Tyler looped his arm around RT's neck, grabbing him into a bear hug as he buried his face in his shoulder. "Son, oh my son. I can't believe it."

An uncomfortable moment passed. RT pushed away a bit, putting himself at arm's length. Tyler eased back into the chair and sat down. Thoughts tumbled through RT's mind like swarming bees he couldn't swat away fast enough. He gulped a deep breath and looked back at Tyler. His lower lip trembled.

Tyler spoke first. "How is this possible? I didn't think I'd ever see you again."

"I didn't think I would see you again either."

"Have you always lived here?"

"For the most part."

"Why didn't you find me before?"

RT felt a wave of defensiveness rise. *Why didn't I find you? A better question might be, Why didn't you find me?* He took a breath to calm himself. "Several years ago, I heard you were in a prison down south. I didn't know if you were still alive."

Tyler's eyes roamed over him, as if searching for some sign of recognition. "When Bob told me to meet his attorney, RT, I never imagined it would be my very own Ryan Tyler."

"Yes. I shortened it when I was in the military. Everyone uses nicknames there."

"You were in the military?"

"Yes." RT struggled to speak. He never imagined he'd meet his dad. He wasn't even sure he'd wanted to. Although he had good memories of his family, the strongest memory of his dad was when he'd been led away in handcuffs. He remembered struggling to get away from the police and seeing his mom crumble into a heap in the middle of the street. He remembered the visits with his mom, and that they never came back for him. He shook his head and squeezed his eyes shut, bringing his mind back to the present. The room grew quiet. When he looked up, Tyler seemed to be studying him.

"Ryan, or rather RT, you can't imagine how happy I am to see you."

RT nodded. "I'm glad to hear that. For years I thought you were mad at me."

Tyler gasped. "Why would you think that?"

"I figured I should have been the one in jail instead of you, and that you must be mad about having to serve my time."

Tyler shook his head, his eyes wide with disbelief. "Why should you have been in jail?"

"I remember how it all happened, every little detail. I was the one looking out for him." He paused. "Noah." After all these years, it was hard to say his name. "I let his head go under."

"You weren't to blame. It was an accident."

"I know that now, but my heart has had a hard time believing that. Guilt has a way of keeping permanent residence in one's soul."

Tyler reached across the table and squeezed RT's hand as tears filled Tyler's eyes. One escaped and rolled down his face. He reached up to swipe it away. "I'm sorry you carried that burden. It was never yours to carry. I'm so sorry."

RT fell quiet again. Tyler filled the silence with another question. "Do you mind my asking why your last name is Ellington?"

"After Mom stopped coming to see me, I was told a family wanted to adopt a boy my age. At the time, I felt so angry. I told them that was fine with me. I figured if you and Mom could leave me, I'd leave you back. I'd go and be another family's son. So, the Ellington's adopted me. Only that didn't end well."

"Why? What happened?" Tyler kept lifting his hand to wipe away tears.

"I didn't want another family. I just wanted you and Mom. I had plenty of anger to dole out. In hindsight, I regret how I treated them. They were only trying to help me, but I didn't want to be helped. I just wanted to be angry."

Tyler slowly shook his head. "We would have never left you son. We were given no choice."

"From my childhood perspective, that's not how it felt, and I'd had some rotten experiences in foster care to fuel that anger. I'd been bounced around, treated badly, and certain it was all my fault. If it hadn't been for the military, I'm not sure where I'd be."

"Yes, the military. How did that come about?" Tyler seemed like a ravished man, hungering for every detail.

"It was at the end of a long, desperate road. I realized if I didn't go into the military, I'd probably end up in jail. The Marines' recruiting office was on my way to work so one day, I just walked in and signed up. After the military worked out my anger and bad attitude, I realized I wanted to help other kids like me. So, I set my sights on getting my law degree."

"What an achievement. I'm so proud of you." Tyler's voice filled with emotion.

"Thanks."

Again, silence filled the room. "So, have you been able to? To help other kids?"

RT's gaze met his father's. "Not as many as I'd like. It's much more complicated than I ever imagined. Children often don't get a voice. Society is quick to judge. No one wants to think of a child being abused or neglected, so if it doesn't affect them personally, they don't want to get involved. It's easier to stand back from a distance and assume CPS is taking care of it."

"I can tell you are very passionate about this."

"I am. I know what it's like to not be heard, to not be asked when decisions are made. People have no idea. There is so much that needs to be done to educate people on what's really going on."

Tyler stood and came around the table. He patted RT on the back. "One thing is certain. You're just the guy to educate them."

The sound of the key being inserted into the lock broke the intensity of the moment. A guard bellowed. "Thornton, your time is up."

Both men rose to their feet and embraced one another. Tyler struggled as he choked back tears. "I've just found you and now I must go. I need more time."

The guard raised an eyebrow as he assessed the situation. Tyler caught his look and chuckled as he whispered. "Guess the guard's never seen a client give his attorney a fatherly hug before."

"Guess they'll have something new to talk about." The edge of RT's mouth lifted into a slight grin.

"Will you come back?"

"Yes. Of course. We have a lot to talk about. I'll plan to come next week and we can talk about where to go from here. Maybe we'll even get around to talking about your case, although I'm probably not the one who should represent you now. It would be a conflict of interest."

Tyler's face lit up. "Oh my gosh. Bob. I can't wait to tell Bob."

RT grinned. "He's never going to believe this."

A slow smile crept onto Tyler's face. "Actually, he just might!"

"Thornton!" The guard grew impatient.

"Coming. I'm coming." He turned to look at RT "I love you son."

RT gave his dad a hug. The guard led Tyler away.

As the door to the room slammed shut, RT whispered, "I love you too, Dad." For years, he'd longed to say that word. Dad. Today it seemed to be stuck in his throat.

47

ASHLEY

As soon as Ashley answered the phone, she could hear excitement in RT's voice. "I have something amazing to tell you."

"You do? I have some pretty remarkable news too."

RT sounded breathless. "Trust me, you need to hear mine first. I've just met my dad."

"What? When?"

"It's a long story, but he's getting out of prison. He'll be out in time for Christmas. I'd like you to meet him. You need to hear his story, especially in your line of work."

"That's amazing RT. I'd love to meet him." She felt a giddy thrill go through her. What an honor he would want her to meet his long-lost father. Although he'd explained his reasoning, she wondered if there was more to it. Did he consider her his girlfriend? Did he want his dad's approval to pursue the relationship further?

RT was still talking. She tried to keep up with his conversation, having gotten lost in her speculative thoughts. "It will be a couple weeks yet, but once he's out, I thought we could meet for breakfast?"

"Sure. That would be fun."

"Great. Let's shoot for Sunday the 20th. We could have a little pre-Christmas celebration. How about we meet at my favorite breakfast spot, Betty's Bakery."

"Great idea. It's one of my favorite spots too."

"Really? Why haven't we ever gone there together?"

"I don't know, but this sounds like a great reason to do it." She loved the way he said the word "together". She'd sure like to do more "together" with him.

"Okay, it's a date." He let out a relaxed laugh.

"I look forward to it. And RT, thank you so much for including me in this special time with your dad."

"Like I said, you have to hear his story."

Her heart sank a bit. So maybe this really was just a professional appointment. Then again... As she hung up the phone, she felt a smile spread across her face. She chuckled a bit, thinking of how, once again, she would wait to tell him about her story. His news definitely trumped her, at least for now, but she needed to share her story soon for fear he'd think she was keeping something from him.

48

TYLER

A week later, when Tyler was escorted to the interview room, his heart felt like it was in his throat. He hoped RT had returned. As he rounded the corner, a slow smile crossed his face. RT was there.

"Good to see you." RT paused and added, "Dad."

Tyler caught his breath. Tears sprang to his eyes. Dad; a word he thought no longer applied to him. "Good to see you too son."

They pulled up chairs and sat across from each other at the table. RT took a deep breath. "So, are you still on track to get out of here in the next few weeks?"

Tyler could tell RT was used to taking control of a conversation. He nodded. "Yes, I'm counting down."

"What are your plans?" RT fumbled with a pen between his fingers.

"I really don't know. I figured I'd get a job, and an apartment. I've had years to ponder that, but to be honest, I'm not really sure where to start."

"Can I help you?"

Tyler hadn't expected that. He stuttered as he tried to respond.

RT held up his hands. "No expectations. Just thought I'd offer."

"That is very kind of you. I'm not used to anyone offering to help me, but I could probably use some." Tyler smiled.

"I have an extra room in my apartment. You could crash there until you're back on your feet." RT paused and then cleared his throat. "Dad?" He cleared his throat again. "What about Mom?"

Tyler grew quiet and looked down at the table. Slowly he raised his head to meet RT's eyes. "I don't know where your mom is." His voice was barely audible.

RT winced. "What? What happened?"

A deep sadness filled Tyler's chest. He never expected he'd have to explain this, especially to his children. He hesitated, searching for the right words. "Oh, I was a fool. I didn't want her to have to wait; to waste her life." He sucked in a sharp breath and exhaled. "We divorced." His face fell into an expressionless mask and his eyes shifted to the floor again. "I'm sorry son. Twenty-five years seemed like forever. It seemed like the right thing at the time."

RT remained quiet. Then his words came out in a sad drawl. "I remember how happy you seemed together. I can't believe you're divorced."

Tyler's voice sounded wistful. "I still love her. I always will. Not a day goes by when I don't think of her. I just hope no matter what she did in her life, she was able to forgive me."

RT reached across the table and squeezed Tyler's hand. "If my memory serves me, she was pretty understanding."

The edge of Tyler's mouth tugged up as he nodded his head. How many times had she shown him mercy? Like when he forgot her birthday, or when he failed to mention friends were coming over after dinner. She didn't let it fluster her although she always made a comment before the lights went out for the night. The next day she would be over it, never carrying a grudge. Of course, that didn't mean he was off the hook. He made sure to bring an extra special gift home the day after he'd forgotten her birthday.

"Dad," RT interrupted his thoughts. "Where'd you go?"

"Oh, just thinking of your mom; such a good woman. I hope she's had a good life."

RT asked the next logical question. "So, what about Leanna? Do you know anything about what happened to her?"

"I was hoping you might know about her Ryan. I mean RT."

"Call me either. It's okay, but no, I don't know anything. I only saw her a couple times after we were taken away. I overheard the caseworker telling Mom I upset Leanna, another thing I felt responsible for. First Noah, then you. I couldn't even help Leanna." RT's words were thick with emotion.

Tyler reached across the table to squeeze RT's hand. "Son, you carried a burden that wasn't yours. It wasn't your fault."

"I know. Trust me. I've spent a considerable amount of money on therapy to help me come to that conclusion, but we need to find them." RT pushed his chair back and stood to his feet.

Tyler chuckled. His son looked ready for battle. "We will. If God allowed me to find you, I know he'll help us find them too." A confidence even he didn't recognize filled his voice. He needed to get something else off his chest. When he spoke, his voice cracked with emotion. "RT, if we find your mom, I'd like to speak to her alone first."

RT nodded. "Of course."

"I need to apologize to her. She'll want to know about you, but I need to make amends. She might have another family by now. She might not want to see me." He paused and looked into his hands that now rested in his lap. Then he looked at RT again. "If I have news of you, at least I will have something to share with her, before she slams the door in my face." He tried to laugh, but it caught in his throat.

"I totally understand." RT paused. " It would be nice to have news of Leanna too. You don't have any idea where she might be?"

"No, I don't. After our parental rights were terminated, we never heard anything. I wasn't sure your mom would live through that. She continued to come see me for years, but I couldn't do anything to help her. I couldn't even hold her to comfort her. If only we hadn't lost you and Leanna. She would have had something."

"Now where was that confidence I heard earlier? Something about God helping us find them?" RT reached down and put his hand on his dad's back.

He lifted his face and smiled. "You're right. Time to focus on the future."

"So, what is the first thing you want to do when you get out?"

"Take a long shower. Alone!"

RT laughed. "I think that can be arranged. Beyond that? A special restaurant? A place you'd like to see?"

"I will be happy just to have time to get to know you, son. That is more than I ever dreamed would happen."

"Again, that can be arranged, and I have someone I want you to meet, so I've already lined up a breakfast date."

"Someone special?" His eyebrows raised in curiosity.

"I guess you could say that." RT stammered a bit. "A friend who needs to hear your story. Anything else I should line up before you get out?"

Tyler grew quiet as his face filled with sadness. "I'd like to see Noah's grave."

RT caught his breath. "Yes, so would I. Do you remember where it is?"

"Yep."

Nothing further was said. When the guard came to escort Tyler to his cell, the men hugged each other goodbye.

"I'll be waiting for you at the gate when you get out Dad."

"Thank you." His voice sounded hoarse.

"Oh, and I left some clothes for you to change into. I hope the sizes are right."

"Much appreciated. I'll be happy to shed this!" He tugged at his orange jumpsuit.

Tyler gave RT a slap on the back and then pulled him into a hug. "See you soon."

49

TYLER

Tyler counted down the hours till his freedom, but as it drew closer, he felt a sense of dread. He never would have guessed he'd struggle with leaving prison, but there was Bob. He changed his life. First, he'd introduced him to Christ and then through a strange twist of fate, connected him to his long-lost son. In the midst of all the uncertainty was a strange peace he'd never felt before. Tyler was still trying to sort it all out.

He knew the guards would come within the hour to escort him out. He needed to somehow say goodbye. He hated that Bob would remain here. He deserved justice, to be cleared of any wrong-doing. Tyler hoped RT was as good an attorney as Bob thought.

Silence filled the cell. Tyler cleared his throat. "I might as well just say it."

Bob looked up from the book he was reading.

"I can't thank you enough Bob. You've changed my life. Thank you for introducing me to RT." His voice wavered.

"Oh, you know that wasn't me. That was all God."

"You're probably right, but He used you to bring us back together."

"I'm so glad that happened."

Tyler felt tears choking in his throat. He'd been raised to believe grown men shouldn't' cry, and yet lately it seemed that's all he did. He swallowed hard, but his voice came out shaky. "Bob, thank you for showing me God loves me, and He never left me. I am ready to start a new journey by getting to know Him better."

211

"It will be the best journey you'll ever take. Find a good Bible teaching church, one that uses scripture for the sermons, not opinions or politics. Get yourself into a small group of other Christians who can help you grow and hold you accountable."

"I will. That's good advice. Thanks."

Bob nodded.

"There's one more thing. It's not right that you're here and your family is suffering as mine did. I want you to know I am going to do everything I can to help clear your name. You don't deserve this; your family doesn't deserve this."

Bob reached over to give Tyler a pat on the back. "Thanks Tyler. I would appreciate anything you could do, more than I can say."

"No problem. We've got our work cut out for us. We need to get the word out. People need to understand their families are at risk of being torn apart and that justice isn't being served. These misunderstandings and wrongful convictions cannot continue."

"I couldn't agree more. No parent should ever have to go through what we have."

Tyler paused. His chin trembled like a bobble head on a dashboard as he held back tears. He put his hand over it. His words came out thick with emotion. "For so long, I thought our family was unique. That it was just our bad luck; then I met you. There are probably others and it's not right."

"No, it's not."

Tyler shook his head and sighed. "I still don't understand why it happened the way it did. I'm glad I met you. If there was a way I could take your place here, I'd do it. Your family is young. I don't want you to lose the years I lost with mine."

Bob's eyes widened. "Tyler, you've already changed. I can't imagine you saying that a few months ago."

"You're right. I wouldn't have, but I can't stand the thought of leaving you here. You deserve to be with your family."

"God is working on that." Bob stood taller as he pushed back his shoulders.

"Man, I admire your faith. I hope mine is that strong someday."

"It already is Tyler. You just haven't tested it out yet. Kick off those training wheels and see where God will take you."

Tyler smiled. He was going to miss Bob. "I'm going to keep my promise to help you, and I know a good attorney who can help too, especially once I'm on the outside." He winked.

"I told you he was good." Bob's voice rose up a notch. "Now go and enjoy your freedom. You've earned yours. Find your girls and make up for lost time."

"I fully intend to." He paused. "I'm not good at this stuff."

Bob filled in the space, "It's not goodbye. We'll be having dinner together with our families soon. You can count on it."

The guard arrived. "Ok Thornton, it's time to leave your luxury hotel."

Tyler smiled. He turned to Bob and gave him a slap on the back. "I'm looking forward to that dinner. I'm buying, so don't take too long or I might change my mind." With a wave to Bob, he made his last journey down the prison halls. It was time for his new beginning.

50

ASHLEY

Ashley felt giddy with excitement as she pulled into the parking lot of Betty's Bakery. She couldn't wait to meet RT's dad and hear about how they met, but she most looked forward to seeing RT. He'd made a way into her heart.

When she entered the restaurant, she saw him sitting at a table with a man. He stood and waved, gesturing for her to join them. She nodded and indicated to the waitress she was with them. As she approached the table, RT gave her an enthusiastic hug and pulled out the chair next to him. Once seated, she reached across the table and extended her hand toward RT's dad. As RT made the introductions, he failed to mention his father's name, simply calling him Dad. Under the circumstances, that was the most important name anyway. Ashley smiled, seeing RT beaming with so much joy.

"Nice to meet you, Ashley." Tyler's words came out a bit halted. He had a funny look on his face. She didn't know what to make of it. She hoped her mascara hadn't smudged or her lipstick slipped off her lips. She rubbed her finger under her eyes and pinched her lips together, just in case. Perhaps she should have checked herself in the bathroom mirror before she came to the table.

RT gushed out his story and Ashley listened in utter amazement. She glanced at Tyler who remained quiet. He smiled, but his eyes were riveted on her. She felt a bit uncomfortable. She averted her eyes back to RT who continued to talk, hardly taking a breath.

After about five minutes, Tyler cleared his throat. "I'm sorry to interrupt you, RT, but I must ask Ashley something."

Ashley looked at RT and then at Tyler. "Sure."

"Do you mind if I ask your age?"

She felt a bit taken back, not certain of the relevance. She didn't want to be rude. She cleared her throat. "I'm twenty-seven. Why do you ask?"

"My daughter Leanna would be twenty-seven. You remind me very much of her mother."

A shiver ran down Ashley's spine. "What did you say your daughter's name is?" Her words came out in a near whisper.

"Leanna."

She felt like someone knocked the wind out of her. Her eyes went wide as she gasped for air. Her body went slack as she leaned into RT.

He put his arm around her. "Ashley, are you okay? You look like you've just seen a ghost."

She didn't look at him. She didn't dare. Instead, she took deep breaths as she focused on Tyler. When the room stopped spinning, her trembling hands reached over to squeeze RT's. She looked back at Tyler. It was him, her father. She couldn't believe it. One more question would confirm it. "What is your last name?"

"Thornton. Why? Is that familiar to you?"

Hot tears flooded her eyes. RT pulled her closer. "Ashley, what is it?"

She turned to look at him. Her voice came out in a whisper as she struggled to speak. "I never told you, RT, but I was a foster child too."

"Seriously?" His eyes went wide. "Wow! How come you never told me?"

"I always meant to, but I preferred to hear about your life and your work. It never seemed to be that important, but it is now."

RT rubbed his chin as a frown crossed his forehead. By now, tears were rolling down Tyler's face. RT looked at his dad and then back to her. "Does someone want to tell me what's going on?"

Her words came out in sobs. "RT, you're my brother."

His mouth dropped open. He seemed to be at a loss for words. She knew she needed to fill in the details. "I've been wanting to learn about my biological family for some time." She gulped in an attempt to control the trembling in her voice. "Last week I found my adoption file." She paused. "My biological parents are Tyler and Sarah Thornton."

RT leaned toward her. "You're Leanna?"

Tyler reached across the table, took her hand, and squeezed it. In a moment, they were all on their feet, arms around each other. Ashley felt like there was no one else in the room as they stood there, arm in arm. Tears streamed down her cheeks. She looked at RT who had a dazed look on his face. Tyler's eyes met hers and he laughed.

At the sound of his laugh, she pulled away and clapped her hand over her mouth. "Oh, my goodness. Did you use to lift me up over your head when I was little?"

He nodded. "Yes, I did. Your giggle brought me so much joy."

"I remember that." She cocked her head.

"How could you? You were so small." A puzzled look crossed Tyler's face.

"I don't know. For as long as I can remember, I've had dreams of a kind man lifting me above his head, hearing his laughter. God must have saved that memory for me all these years."

Ashley felt like she might collapse if she didn't sit. The men took their seats too. The waitress came over to take their order. Since none of them even looked at the menu, RT ordered the first thing on the menu for all of them. Ashley could have cared less. Food was the last thing on her mind, but they should at least order something.

Tyler spoke up first. "Now more than ever, we need to find your mom. You really do look like her, Ashley. When I saw you, I felt like I'd stepped back in time."

"You don't know where she is?" Ashley didn't understand.

The men filled her in. Ashley felt like she was on an emotional teeter-totter as she looked from one man to the other, unable to take her eyes off them. From the ecstasy of meeting her dad, to the shock in realizing RT was her brother, to the sadness in not knowing what became of her mother. The thought of not finding her caused tears to well again in her eyes.

Tyler's voice was tender. "Ashley, we'll find her. I think I know where to start. In the meantime, I'd really love to hear about your life."

For the duration of the meal, Ashley told them about her life. Tyler asked numerous questions. RT didn't say a word, but watched her the entire time she talked. She took a drink of water and then turned to RT. "You're awfully quiet."

He shook his head. "Why didn't I put it together before? I guess I didn't know you were adopted, but still." He put his arm around her and gave her another hug. "Hey little sis, you have grown into a beautiful woman."

She blushed and returned his hug. She started to giggle.

"What?" RT looked confused all over again.

"I was just thinking. Aren't you glad we never kissed?"

With that, both of them burst out laughing.

51

TYLER

Tyler drove by their family home several times. On one occasion he noticed small children walking toward the house. He figured Sarah must not live there anymore. Today though, he had a purpose. He had to find her. She would want to know about Ryan and Leanna, even if she didn't want to see him, and he didn't know where else to start.

He pulled into the neighborhood and parked the car next to the curb across from their old house. He wanted to watch for a while. Perhaps he'd recognize a neighbor. If not, he'd knock on doors until he found someone who knew where she moved.

For just a moment, he allowed his mind to wander back to happier days when he and Ryan used to toss a baseball in the front yard, and Leanna learned to ride her tricycle on the sidewalk. Looking at the house that had once been theirs, he felt a warmth in his heart. It looked weathered, yet still painted yellow with white trim, the colors they painted it when they first moved in. The oak tree that could only support a small child's swing had grown into a mighty oak that now shaded the front porch.

He closed his eyes, breathing in the crisp air of winter. He could hear the chatter of children, the sound of a bicycle bell on a child's bike, the scraping of a skateboard coming to a halt, and the sound of a basketball bouncing on the pavement. Oh, the sounds of life, of children, of the life he'd been denied.

The next sound he heard caused his heart to skip a beat. His eyes popped open. It was the sound of her voice.

52

SARAH

It had been a long day at work. As Sarah pulled into her driveway and pushed the garage door opener, a ball bounced into the driveway. She slammed on the brakes, hoping to avoid any child who might be following it. Putting her car into park, she stepped out.

The little boy from next door rushed over to her. "I'm sorry Miss Sarah. I didn't mean for it to bounce into your driveway."

"Oh, it's ok Nate." She leaned to pick up the ball and toss it back to him. "Here you go."

"Thanks Miss Sarah."

She waved as he went off to play again. As she started to get back into her car, she felt a strange sense of being watched. Pausing, she turned toward the street. She gasped. Tyler. She would know him anywhere, even after all these years.

He was walking toward her, but when their eyes met, he stopped. Without thinking she started walking toward him, hcr pace quickening with each step. She could feel a smile spread across her face. Tyler continued moving toward her, matching his pace to hers. The years dissolved as they crashed into each other's arms.

53

TYLER

Tyler didn't want to release the hug, but he had to see her face. He took a step back and looked at her. Her eyes glistened as tears filled the corners.

He spoke first. "You look as beautiful as always."

She bit her lip as she shook her head side to side. "I can't believe you're here."

"Sorry I took so long." A sly smile crept onto his face.

Her eyes smiled in return, then she seemed to snap back to reality. "Oh, my goodness. What are we doing standing here in the street? Can you come in? Do you have time to visit? I could make dinner." Her eyes searched his face.

"That's the best offer I've had in twenty-five years. So yes. Definitely yes."

"We have a lot to catch up on." Her voice was tentative.

"We certainly do, and I've got a little surprise for you."

Her eyes narrowed. He laughed.

"What?" Her eyes popped open.

"Oh, how I've missed that look Sarah. Do you know how many times I thought of that look of yours through the years?" He couldn't wipe the smile from his face.

"Evidently not enough." A playful pout replaced the smile. She reached out to touch his arm. It felt like electricity shot through it. The tingle remained even after she took her hand away. "Let's go inside. I'll park the car in the garage and get dinner going."

He followed her in like a lost puppy. He couldn't take his eyes off her. Her hair had a few streaks of gray, but otherwise, she looked just as he remembered. He didn't think he'd held up as well. His dark hair long ago lost its color. She didn't seem to notice as she went about making fried chicken, talking and asking questions, but he didn't want to talk. He just wanted to take it in, to hear her voice, to watch her, to continue pinching himself to make sure he wasn't dreaming. This wasn't how he thought she'd receive him.

He moved to stand beside her as she turned the fried chicken. "Can I help?"

Her hands stopped moving as she turned to look at him. "Tyler Thornton. What has happened to you? Helping in the kitchen was never your thing."

"That was before I realized how special every moment was with you." He fought the urge to put a kiss on those lips of hers, but he didn't want to rush things.

She took a step back and looked him in the face. A slight smile tugged at her lips. Oh man, why did she have to do that? The urge to kiss her only magnified.

He stepped away to wash his hands in the kitchen sink, so familiar and yet, more of a memory. When he turned back around, she handed him two plates along with silverware. "You can set the table. Then I want you to sit and tell me everything that has happened."

"I'm happy to set the table, but I'd prefer to hear everything that has happened to you first. My days were pretty much the same."

Her eyes softened. "I'll bet. Okay, I'll share first."

She carried a plate of fried chicken to the table. He followed her with bowls of boiled potatoes and steamed green beans. His mouth watered already. She reached for his hand. "May I say a blessing?"

"Yes, of course." He didn't hear a word she said as he watched her bow her head, observed her lips moving, and felt her smooth hand in his. It made his heart ache to think of all the days he'd missed with her.

Over dinner, she told him about her work at the hospital, how she'd gone back to school to get her nursing license, and the changes in the neighborhood. It was mostly surface subjects. Stuff friends talk about. Then she told him of her parents' passing. He offered his condolences. Once again, he regretted he hadn't been there for her, a familiar regret. He hadn't been there for his parents either when they fell ill and died.

After dinner, they moved into the living room. He sat in a leather chair and she sat on the couch. She had updated the furniture, all except the wooden rocking chair. It was still in the corner by the bookshelf just as it had been when they lived here as a family. She'd also put tan wall-to-wall carpet in, a huge improvement over the orange shag rug. His eyes teared up as he stepped back in time, visualizing this room where their children used to watch movies and play. He cleared his throat. "I like the changes you've made."

"Thanks. Things wear out after twenty-five years."

He nodded and cleared his throat again. "Sarah, I need to apologize." He looked at her, but she didn't move an inch. "I was wrong to push you away. I thought it best." He paused. "I was a fool. I am so very sorry. I hope you can forgive me."

She didn't make eye contact. Her lips twitched, but she didn't speak right away. When she did, her words came out with thoughtful heaviness. "I must admit. I was very angry at you." She turned to look at him. "Tyler, you broke my heart."

His hands were shaking. "I know. I can't tell you how sorry I am."

She nodded. "Me too. Thank you for your apology. It was long overdue." He looked at the floor, waiting for her to finish. He deserved whatever wrath she might pour out on him.

She allowed her words to sit in the silence, then she said what she'd rehearsed for so many years. "It took me a long time to forgive you, but I did. Too much of our lives have been lost to the past. I don't want to go there anymore. Let's focus on what's ahead."

Tyler leaned back in his chair, closed his eyes, and let out a deep breath. Again, her response was unexpected. In his decades in prison, he had given up on the idea there could ever be a future with Sarah. He didn't deserve it. Tears stung at the back of his eyes. "Sarah, I can't tell you how much I appreciate you saying that." He couldn't say more, overcome with emotion.

Sarah stood and without saying a word, moved to the desk and returned with an aged envelope. She handed it to him.

"What is this?"

"Our divorce papers."

He gulped.

"I never filed them." He looked up at her with wide eyes. She continued. "I thought it was worth waiting for you to see if you really wanted this."

He felt light-headed and put his hands on the chair arms, fearing he'd fall off the chair. His face paled. "What? We're not divorced?"

She shook her head. "I told you I would wait for you."

His voice went up a pitch. "You mean we're still married?"

"If you want to be."

Every shred of composure he'd been keeping in check collapsed as tears ran down his face. "I can't believe it. Nothing would make me happier than being a part of your life again."

"We don't have to decide now, but I thought you should know."

He nodded and whispered, "Thank you."

He knew he needed to tell her about the children, but he had to collect himself first. Sarah remained silent as she watched him from the couch.

He cleared his throat. "I have a surprise for you too."

The corner of her mouth tipped up. "You hinted at that earlier."

He nodded, still trying to recover from the shock that he was still married to her.

"Are you going to tell me?" She leaned forward and wrinkled her nose.

He smiled. No wonder he never stopped loving this woman, a treasure that had not diminished over time.

"It's about the children. I have found them. Or I should say, God has found them for us."

Sarah's hand flew over her mouth as she gasped. "What? How?" Now it was her turn to cry.

He laughed again. It had been years since he'd laughed this much. For the next hour, he shared the miracle of their children and how God's hand had been on them. He told her of his newfound love for Jesus. Then late in the evening, they called RT and Ashley so Sarah could talk to them. Plans were made to meet the following day.

The excitement wore them both out. It was time to call it a day, but he didn't want to go. He didn't want to leave her. She must have felt the same as she motioned toward the back porch. "Let's move outside. It's a beautiful evening."

The winter evening air felt brisk, but fresh air was much needed. Tyler needed to clear his mind. As they moved onto the porch, a slight breeze pushed a hanging porch swing, another addition since he'd been gone. "I like the new porch swing."

"Me too. I've spent many evenings here thinking of all of you. Let's sit."

They both sat on opposite ends of the swing. They allowed it to carry them in silence. Sarah started to shiver. "It's chilly. I'll get a blanket." She stood, rubbed her hands up and down her arms, and went inside to retrieve one.

When she returned, she brought a thick down-filled blanket, large enough for the two of them. She sat closer to him this time. He felt her warmth. It warmed his body. He lifted his arm to wrap it around her shoulders and pulled her closer. She didn't resist as she placed her head on his shoulder. His heart skipped a beat. A sense of joy overtook every inch of his soul. This felt so right. They were together, as they always should have been.

Soon it got quiet between them, he glanced down at her. She had fallen asleep. He tucked the blanket closer and pulled her tight into his side. Putting his face to her hair, he breathed deeply. He felt intoxicated with happiness. He closed his eyes. Soon he too was asleep with Sarah in his arms.

54

ASHLEY

A month passed since their unbelievable reunion. Ashley couldn't help smiling as she looked around this intimate circle of people. Her mom Becky was on her right. Her mom Sarah was on her left. Across from her were Tyler and RT. Over the past month, they met many times one-on-one and together as a group, trying to make up for lost time. They wept thinking of the many things they missed: birthday parties, graduations, the first days of school, piano recitals, swim meets, and even small things like waiting for the tooth fairy. It was time they could never recover. There was tremendous grief in that, but they also knew they had so much to be grateful for, since they found each other. There would be many days ahead to celebrate.

In the past month, Ashley gave notice at her job and took a new position working with families in crisis. She was helping them learn new skills so they could function as a healthy family before becoming a part of the foster care system.

RT continued to work defending Bob as well as a few new clients. Whenever he caught her eye, he would wink. After their shocking reunion, he confessed. "You know, you would have been a great girlfriend, but you're an even better sister." She felt privileged in getting to know him in the past months. It gave them a head start in making up for lost time.

Her dad found a job as a mechanic at a local garage, grateful to have his hands busy. Technology for vehicles changed in the past twenty-five years but he loved to learn and it felt good to be productive again.

Sarah, on the other hand, decided to retire. Through the years, she paid off the mortgage and saved a little money. In light of her recent life changes, she expressed the desire to have more time. Ashley already found her two moms, on more than one occasion, sharing a pot of coffee and going through her childhood scrapbooks.

So much had changed, but today wasn't about the past. It was about moving forward together as a family, and there was no better place to gather than here. Here at Noah's grave.

A slight breeze tugged at the hem of Ashley's skirt. She reached to take both of her mother's hands and squeezed them, taking a moment to look each of them in the eyes. How she loved them both. She was grateful her mom took the news so well and in her typical manner, embraced her biological family, making room for them in her life.

It was quiet as they shared this solemn moment together, listening to the sound of the wind through the trees.

Tyler spoke first, his voice trembling. "I'd like to take a moment and offer a prayer of thanksgiving." His eyes met each person individually. They nodded in agreement. "Heavenly Father, You are amazing. I gave up on you so long ago. I turned my back, thinking you failed me, and yet, what a gift you gave us. I have so many regrets for the life and time I missed. Today, Lord, you put the pieces of our lives back together again.

Thank you for keeping my beautiful wife for me, for filling her with so much love that she never left me, and for keeping her safe during these years. I thank you for your earthly angels in Becky and Tom who made sure our little Leanna was loved and cared for. Now she is this beautiful woman in Ashley. And although I am grieved over the hardships RT went through, I thank you that you used them to cause him to become an attorney with a passion for the innocent.

Had it not been for that, we might never have found each other again." He paused as he struggled to continue.

A moment passed. Her mom Becky picked up the prayer, "Lord, it is an honor to be standing in this circle, with this sweet and precious family. As I look at each of these faces, I see a testament of your faithfulness. Although my heart breaks for what they went through, I know you will not let those trials be wasted. You will use them as you are doing now, to bring joy, to sustain us in trials, and to create wonderful memories. I thank you for giving us Ashley. She was always your child on loan to us. Thank you that we were able to love and protect her in a season when her own family were denied such joys."

Quiet sobs filled the air.

Tyler gathered himself, ready to continue. "Lord, who would have guessed you would take this broken man, serving time in prison, and make him whole again. Thank you for Bob who showed me your love. In time, I pray that all who gather in this circle will call you Lord. You have performed a miracle in our family by bringing us back together."

RT cleared his throat and began to speak, "I really don't know who I am talking to because long ago, I gave up on there being a God. I also recognize we aren't here by coincidence. It could only be divine intervention. Maybe even as Dad has said, a miracle. So, if this is the work of God Almighty, then I acknowledge you and thank you for bringing our family back together."

Tyler sucked in a sob as he reached to hug RT in a gripping squeeze. He whispered, "Thank you God for revealing yourself to my son. Thank you, God."

Sarah moved to hug her men. She too prayed, "Lord, please forgive me for doubting you, for thinking my prayers were pointless, and for losing hope. You have done a mighty thing for us. We don't deserve your grace and kindness, but we accept it with thankful hearts. Thank you for your promise of a glorious reunion you revealed to me in church just weeks ago. I had no idea. You truly are a God of miracles. And Noah. Although I don't think I can ever accept our sweet boy..." Her voice caught a sob. She took a moment to gather herself and continued. "I don't think I can ever understand why our Noah was taken from us so early, but I know he is with you in heaven. I know we will be with him someday. Thank you for bringing our family back together. Help me learn to trust you more."

Without saying a word, her mom Becky slowly made her way around the circle and gently laid her hand on each person's head. Although no one could hear her words, her lips moved in silent prayer. She rejoined the circle, again taking Ashley's hand.

Ashley's heart felt like it might overflow. She was filled with gratitude as she added her prayer. "Lord, you have taught me so much, given me so much. Every step of my life has led me to this point. Since Dad's death, I have felt such a longing to find my biological family. Against all odds, you made that happen. As grateful as I am for both my fathers and both my mothers, I know you are my one true Father. We have missed so much together, but you were with each of us every minute. There will never be enough time to make up for what we've lost, but for whatever time we have, we commit it to you. Make me worthy Lord, of your gracious gifts."

Again, soft sobs filled the air. Sarah broke the circle of hands and took a step toward Noah's grave, leaving a yellow daisy on his headstone. Each member of the family followed suit. They again gathered in a circle, this time around Noah's headstone.

It was Tyler who completed the prayer, "Lord, our sweet Noah is a reminder of how a tragedy can cause misunderstanding and wrongful convictions. Protect the children who truly are being abused or neglected. Find them loving parents like Tom and Becky. For those parents or caregivers who have been wrongly accused, bring forth a cloud of witnesses to declare their innocence. We especially pray for Bob. Thank you for allowing me the opportunity to meet him. Thank you for giving him a bold faith, even in prison.

You used him to change our lives. You used him to bring us together again. It is an example of how you will use the most tragic of circumstances for our good and your glory. Lord, we trust Bob's future to you. You have given us a new purpose in helping him. Show us how we can best support him until his name is cleared and he is reunited with his family. Thank you, Lord. We give you all the honor and praise. Amen."

"Amen," they all said in unison.

There wasn't a dry eye among them as they raised their eyes and looked at one another. Smiles spread around the group. Ashley giggled, and soon they were all laughing as they embraced each other. It was time to start over, to begin again as a family, each changed in ways they could never have anticipated.

As the group started to move apart, she noticed Tyler pull Sarah into his arms. Ashley didn't want to intrude and yet, something drew her there, watching.

Tyler leaned to kiss Sarah. He spoke just loudly enough that Ashley could overhear. "Sarah, thank you for waiting for me. I intend to fulfill my promise to be your husband until death. You are, and will always be, the only girl I will ever kiss."

EPILOGUE

Now that you've read *For The Children*, you might have a few questions like: What happened to Bob? Was he cleared and reunited with his family? And little Michael? Did another family adopt him? Or the grandma who left the note? Did she ever find her granddaughter? What about the Acer children? If these are your questions, then thank you! That's what I hoped because the world is full of children and families with unfinished stories; stories that are waiting to be heard and validated.

As a mother of three young adult children, two of whom we adopted from the foster care system, I have the greatest respect for the diligent CPS workers who rescue and advocate for children. They have one of the toughest jobs imaginable. Despite their amazing work, the system is broken and as a result, families and children are suffering.

My realization of this brokenness came after friends were wrongly accused of Shaken Baby Syndrome (or Abusive Head Trauma) and forced to relinquish their infant to CPS. It made no sense. They would never hurt their child. Yet, the injustice they endured as a result of the false accusation was astounding.

Because of their experience, I began doing research on the child welfare system. The more I learned, the more horrified I became. God laid it upon my heart to write this book to help raise awareness of these issues.

Although this is a fictional story, many families in America are living these scenarios in real life. They are stuck as they wait for exoneration, wait to be reunited with their families, wait for justice, and wait for child welfare reform. They are real live people living out real life horrors, just like the Thornton family. Unlike the Thorntons in *For The Children*, many families are never reunited. The trauma of separation and loss impacts them for the rest of their lives and often affects generations that follow.

In the comfort of our culture, it is easy to lull ourselves into thinking American children are being taken care of, because we have a system in place to protect them. In many cases, nothing could be farther from the truth. The facts are:

➢ Children are suffering from every atrocity imaginable at the hands of their own parents, AND children are dying while under the protection of CPS.

➢ Children are allowed to remain or be reunited with known abusive parents, AND children are being taken from loving parents, sometimes without a warrant or proof of abuse or neglect.

➢ Children are being cared for and loved in licensed foster homes, AND children are being abused and mistreated in foster homes.

➢ Children are being treasured and loved in adoptive homes, AND children are discarded into treatment programs because there is nowhere else for them to go.

➢ Children are being bounced from foster homes to group homes, never finding permanence, AND children have been lost to the system when extended families are willing to love and care for them.

➢ The spectrum of abuse and neglect of children is staggering. It is being done to them by their own parents, by foster parents, group homes, by the agency formed to protect them, and in some cases, by the judicial system.

Our children are at tremendous risk. As a result, our very culture is at risk because what we do for our children is a reflection of our culture as a whole.

God is very clear about the role of children in our world. In Psalm 127:3, Scripture says, "Children are a gift from the Lord. They are a reward from Him." (NLT). The Message translation is even more direct: "Don't you see that children are God's best gift?"

Jesus frequently referenced children in his analogies. When describing the essence of salvation, He called a child to Him and said, "I'm telling you, once and for all, that unless you return to square one and start over like children, you're not even going to get a look at the kingdom, let alone get in. Whoever becomes simple and elemental again, like this child, will rank high in God's kingdom." (Matthew 18:3- 4 Message version).

Children are very important to God. Yet whether it is in America or third-world countries, children are the most mistreated population. They are used as suicide bombers, are violated, abused, sold or given into sex slavery, trafficked, or given away in childhood marriages. They are victimized, sacrificed, and killed for political causes and personal convenience. Our children are being robbed of their childhoods and in some cases, their very lives, even in America.

Today in America, there are more children in foster care than ever before. They are living in temporary situations as they struggle to find a place to belong. Their cry? "I just want to be wanted." For many children, the course of their lives could be changed by one caring person who chose to invest in them, even if only for a short time.

Please join me in taking an active role to help create solutions to protect our most vulnerable citizens. May I suggest one of the following:

➢ Consider being a safe, loving foster home for a child in need.

- ➢ Come alongside a foster family by providing meals, respite care, prayers, and financial assistance.
- ➢ Help a struggling family so children don't end up in foster care.
- ➢ Stand in the gap for a family who has been wrongly accused.
- ➢ Come alongside a grandparent who is raising grandchildren.
- ➢ Sponsor a child overseas or in a children's home.
- ➢ Encourage a single mom to help her family together.
- ➢ Volunteer at a safe house so families can learn to live sober and healthy lives.
- ➢ Support teen crisis centers so teens have a way out of sex trafficking and homelessness.
- ➢ Support crisis pregnancy centers to help expecting mothers choose life and adoption rather than abortion.
- ➢ Encourage parenting education in schools where young adults can learn to make healthy decisions before they become parents.
- ➢ Advocate for children by testifying for and promoting legislation that puts children before politics and profits.
- ➢ Adopt a child who is not in a safe biological home or a young adult who has aged out and would like to belong to a family.
- ➢ Mentor a pregnant teen or help a teen crisis center.
- ➢ Be informed and available to help children and families in crisis.
- ➢ Answer Christ's call to be his hands and feet for the orphans in the world.

As a mother, I am painfully aware it could have been my children who never found a home, who ended up abused or neglected, or who slipped through the cracks. To be blunt, it could have been yours as well. Children don't choose to lose parents to drugs, addictions, wrongful accusations, or death any more than children choose parents who have good jobs, stable marriages, and lives free of trauma. So, for one moment, visualize your child or family member in a stranger's home, or on the streets, or being passed around as a commodity for sex or drugs. Would you do something then? Would you step forward? Would you speak up? If so, then I challenge you to do that! We can't afford to turn a blind eye simply because it hasn't happened to us. We can't continue to do nothing to preserve our own orderly world. The time to act is now. If we don't, we might find our children or grandchildren victims of a tragedy that should never happen.

For The Children was written to raise awareness of the vastness and complexity of social issues children are facing. In raising awareness, I hope to give a voice to the thousands of children who are not in a safe, permanent home and challenge us to be agents for change. Most important, it was written to remind us in this world of brokenness, **God is the Great Restorer.** He is the healer of broken relationships and broken people. So, if you are broken (and most of us are), know God is always with you, working on your behalf for your good and His glory. You are, after all, His beloved child.

Please share this book with others and engage in the following discussion or on my website: <u>**www.DeniseEJohnson.com**</u> where you will also find a promotional book trailer that can be shared on social media (https://vimeo.com/203882374). I would also appreciate it if you could write a review on Amazon.com, even if you didn't purchase through Amazon. Use this novel, *For The Children*, as a way to start conversations about this critical issue in our country. Most importantly, decide how you will use your gifts, desires, talents, and connections to advocate for children and families in crisis. Determine to take your place in serving our greatest treasure or, as God put it, our "best gift". Choose to be part of the solution because, this story could have been yours.

Thank you for reading *For the Children*,
Denise E. Johnson

Denise E. Johnson

DISCUSSION FOR
BOOK CLUBS OR BIBLE STUDIES:

Chapters 1 – 5

- Have you ever known someone who has been personally or professionally involved in foster care? Share your experiences without disclosing confidential information.
- If you thought someone was being abused or neglected (adult or child), what would you do? Mind your own business? Pretend not to notice? Call the authorities? Confront the abuser? Other ideas?
- What would you consider abuse? What would you consider neglect? What is the difference? If in a group, are you hearing a difference of opinion? Consider in America, most children (80%) are removed due to neglect, not abuse.
- Do you think what is considered neglect could be subjective? For example, allowing a child to walk home alone. Could circumstances determine if it's neglect or abuse? Could an unkempt house be considered neglect?
- When faced with helping a friend through tragedy, what are positive ways to respond?
- If you've experienced grief, what did you find to be the most productive way to get through that season? What are ways others meant for comfort that might have actually brought pain?
- Call your local hospital to find out how many infants are born with drug addictions and what happens to them. Do they need help rocking babies?

Denise E. Johnson

Chapters 6 – 10

- Were you or anyone you loved ever in an accident when no one was to blame? Have you ever been wrongly accused of something (hitting your little sister, shoplifting)? How did you feel? Did it change your life in any way? Are there accidents that warrant consequences like jail? Are there accidents that don't? What's the difference?
- With our world of demands, schedules, and appointments, how quickly or willingly would you be able to help a neighbor in need? Do you currently know of someone who needs help that you aren't helping even though you could?
- Imagine a house fire or other disaster destroying your home. Describe how you would feel living in another place, wearing someone else's clothes, wondering when you would have a home again? Consider how foster children feel.
- Have you ever been in a situation where you felt completely helpless? How did you cope? Who did you call? What resources did you lean on to get through the crisis? Are you a resource for others? Who, in your circle of relationships, knows you would be there for them? Who is there for you?

Chapters 11 – 15

- Have you ever been in a courtroom or before a judge? How did you feel? Would you have enough knowledge from watching TV dramas to know what to expect if you were the accused of a crime? Note: What you see on TV is generally criminal vs. family court.
- Were you ever separated from your parents, even for a short time, like being lost in the department store? How did you feel while you were lost? How did you feel when you were reunited?
- Have you ever considered that some adoptions don't go well, that children are returned to the system? For a child, it might feel a bit like a jilted wife when learning her husband has a new love. How would a child process these feelings? What might they determine about themselves? How might this affect future relationships?

Chapters 16 – 20

- Imagine being told you would need to live in another home from now on. Your new home would be nicer, cleaner, and would have a maid. The only catch was you couldn't be with anyone you knew. How would you feel about this? Which life would you prefer?
- I don't think any of us could think of anything worse than having our children taken from us. Consider for a moment that the number one risk factor for a child being removed from their home is poverty. Does that seem appropriate? Discuss why this is happening and how it could create a domino effect in families and communities.
- Have you ever been in a situation that felt like it would never end? That it would never get better or seemed hopeless? Discuss how you worked through this.
- Have you ever had to play by a set of rules you thought were unfair? Have you ever been required to do something that went against your own moral beliefs?

Chapters 21 – 25

- Does it seem far-fetched that Sarah lost her children as a result of Tyler's plea agreement? Had you ever heard of this happening? Check out Sanders vs. DPS Michigan. Other states have laws that penalize the non-offending parent. Does this seem like the best interests of the child and/or family?
- Have you experienced or known someone who struggles with an addiction(s)? How do you feel watching them? How do you think they feel? Is it a disease or a choice? This is an interesting read on the subject: Surgeon General Vivek Murthy: Addiction Is A Chronic Brain Disease, Not A Moral Failing | HuffPost Life.
- When you think of foster children, what sort of images go through your mind? What kinds of questions would you want to ask a foster child? Consider that often children are asked, "What did you do that made you go into foster care?" How would this make a child feel?

Chapters 26 – 30

- Have you ever visited someone in prison or jail? Have you ever considered serving the prison population? What are ways one could serve them? Consider calling a local prison to find out how to help.
- Have you ever experienced trauma? Something that changed your life or your view of life? Do you remember how you felt, reacted? How old were you? Nightmares, fears, other long-term results? What steps did you take to heal from the trauma?
- Do you know anyone who is adopted? Have you considered what the biological family must think about as the years pass? What about the adoptive family; what things do they ponder as their child grows up? Do you think you could give up a child for adoption if you knew you couldn't take care of them? When you think of adoption, does it elicit any positive or negative feelings? Or curiosities?

Chapters 31 – 35

- Did you ever let go of a relationship (for any reason)? Do you still think of them on occasion? Do you have regrets? Were you able to move on and find peace without the relationship? How did you do it and what did you learn?
- Look up sunshineacres.org and palmerhome.org. What do these homes offer for children? Look up safe-families.org or Promise686.org. How are they different from state run foster care? (The average foster child in CPS care stays in the system two years).
- Find out how many homeless teens are in your community (local high schools should know). Is there something you could do to help? Donate food, clothing, gloves, hats, personal items.
- Are you aware that homeless teens are targets for sex trafficking? How can you intercede for vulnerable teens? Is there an organization in your community that serves teens?

- Do grandparents have rights to see their grandchildren in your state?

-Chapters 36 – End

- What are some of your favorite Christmas memories? What traditions has your family carried on? What meaning do they have for you? Are traditions important for children?
- Do you believe in a God who cares about the details of your life? Have you ever felt like giving up on God? Or that God gave up on you?
- Have you ever experienced what you would consider a miracle; something that couldn't be explained by logic or ordinary circumstances?
- Have you ever heard the still small voice of God? What did He say?
- Describe the most wonderful reunion you've ever had. Perhaps a loved one home from deployment? A child found after being lost? What were your feelings?
- Are you aware that over 400,000 children are in the foster care system, more than ever recorded? Did you know of the children rescued from sex trafficking, over 65% report having been a foster child? What can you personally do to help children in crisis? Brainstorm ideas and organize a group activity to serve children in need.
- Watch the 2016 movie called *Lion*. Identify what population of children you most identify with (country, age, gender, etc.) and decide how you will personally help children in crisis. If each of us does a little, we can change the tide and help children to be recognized as the gift they are.
- Watch the movie *The Syndrome*. Is it possible that science can be manipulated to benefit a specific agenda?
- Watch the movie based on a true story, *Take Care of Maya*.

Thank you for reading *For The Children*. I hope it helped raise awareness of the crisis children and families face in our country and inspired you to become involved in advocacy for children.

Please consider writing a review on Amazon, share the promotional video For The Children, a novel written by Denise E. Johnson on Vimeo at: https://vimeo.com/203882374, recommend the book to others, and most importantly, be a voice for our children.

Blessings, Denise Johnson

Website: www.DeniseEJohnson.com